THE TIGER THAT SWALLOWED THE BOY

THE TIGER THAT SWALLOWED THE BOY

Exotic Animals in Victorian England

John Simons

LIBRI
PUBLISHING

Copyright © Libri Publishing 2012

ISBN 978 1 907471 71 1

The right of John Simons to be identified as the author of this work has been asserted in accordance with the Copyright, Designs and Patents Act, 1988.

A CIP catalogue record for this book is available from The British Library

Cover design by Helen Taylor

Design by Carnegie Publishing

Printed in the UK by Ashford Colour Press

Index by James Lamb: james@jalamb.com

Libri Publishing
Brunel House
Volunteer Way
Faringdon
Oxfordshire
SN7 7YR

Tel: +44 (0)845 873 3837

www.libripublishing.co.uk

Contents

Illustrations

Preface & Acknowledgements

Books are like quarries in that when you write one (or dig one) you end up with a book (or quarry) and a spoil heap. Sometimes there is a lot of good stuff in the spoil heaps – the silver in the spoil heaps from the lead mines just outside Aberystwyth for example – and it seems a shame to waste it. This book is one of two that have been dug from the spoil heap of my *Rossetti's Wombat* which came out in 2008 and was largely concerned with the specifics of the Pre-Raphaelite painter and poet Dante Gabriel Rossetti's private menagerie and, more generally, with the Australian animals who crowded the streets of Victorian London and filled the fields of the English countryside in surprising numbers and with vigour and exuberance. Out of the spoil heap came a short cultural history of kangaroos and this larger study of exotic animals in Victorian England. Victorian England means just that and the main focus of the book is on the years 1837 to 1901. There is, of course, some address to the presence of exotic animals in earlier periods in things like the Tower and Exeter 'Change menageries and the early years of the touring and private menageries. But this is simply to show how the *tsunami* of exotic animals which deluged England in the nineteenth century was the product of a gently lapping tide that had been rising since the Middle Ages. In the nineteenth century it became catastrophic due to a fortuitous combination of Imperial adventure and expansion and the discovery of education and science as tools of political reform and social control.

This book ranges over both familiar and unfamiliar territory and concentrates on the unfamiliar. For example, it doesn't spend as much time on London Zoo as it might have done as that zoo's history has been written extensively in many other places but it does look at Manchester's Belle Vue Zoo in some depth. Lord Walter Rothschild's menagerie at Tring is also given relatively short treatment partly because it was less important as a menagerie than as a museum and partly because Lord Walter has been the subject of a substantial biographical monograph which gives extensive treatment to the museum and menagerie – which did, after all, define his life. Tring is treated very much as a point of comparison with the earlier and equally influential although now less known collection of Lord Edward Stanley, Earl of Derby, at Knowsley Hall and to illustrate the ways in which the shape and motivations of zoological collections and collectors in the nineteenth century were not uniform but were sculpted by the larger social forces that played around them. Earl Fitzwilliam's menagerie at Wentworth Woodhouse was, although much smaller than the Knowsley collection, as important in its own way as an example of the serious zoological intent and the genuine interest in the animals shown by its owner.

The book tries to trace the complete cycle of the exotic animal phenomenon in Victorian England. Significant attention is paid to the trade in animals and, in particular, the business structure of the Jamrach family firm, which dominated the English trade for the second half of the nineteenth century, is set out in detail, I believe for the first time. Attention is then given, in turn, to the various locations in which exotic animals could be seen: the zoological gardens, the private menagerie, the circus, the travelling menagerie and the natural history museum. Although the focus is on England and to a lesser extent Scotland and Ireland I also spend some time looking at the opportunities to encounter exotic animals across the Empire and specifically, in Australia. This is for four reasons. The first is that the citizens of the Australian colonies thought of themselves as British. This is not to say that by the end of the nineteenth century there wasn't a specifically Australian identity but that people there broadly looked to the "Old Country" (a phrase you still sometimes hear from elderly Australians) for all manner of things and not least culture and entertainment. The second is that since the spoil heap for this book first piled up on my desk I have moved to live in Australia and all my work now reflects that new context. The third is that Australia was one of the few Imperial domains over which Britain had a complete monopoly. This gave the Australian bird and animal trade a particularly important role which was different in quality and scale from, say, the trade in Canadian animals which was more or less entirely based around the whaling and fur (beaver, bear and seal) industries and led to the near extinction of the beaver and Canadian bison. The fourth is that the underlying thesis of this book is that the exotic animal industry was intimately related to the contours of Empire and Imperialism and that to understand it fully you have to take an Imperial perspective. That there is a relationship between animals and Empire is not, of course, a new idea and was authoritatively articulated by

Harriet Ritvo some twenty-five years ago. What I am doing here is building a very detailed picture of some aspects of it and showing how those details were conditioned by the specific opportunities that Empire made possible – or which the decline of Empire closed off.

During the writing of this book two interesting novels appeared both of which relate to its theme. The first, Christopher Nicholson's *The Elephant Keeper*, is a wonderful evocation of the world of the private menageries of the eighteenth century and although it isn't based on fact it could well be. The second, *Jamrach's Menagerie* by Carol Birch, is a good yarn based very loosely indeed on the incident of the escaped tiger which is a key structural element of this book. The real story is a good deal stranger.

All of this work has been written at Macquarie University in Australia and I acknowledge the support of my colleagues there especially Professor Judyth Sachs and my Vice Chancellor Professor Steven Schwartz. It had its origins in Lincoln University and, in particular, I would like to mention the Lincoln University students, now graduates, Paul Day and Tony Pollard, who were recipients of that university's undergraduate research awards and spent their scholarships working with me to build a database of travelling menageries and helping me plot their course around the British Isles during Queen Victoria's reign.

I must acknowledge my wife Kathryn, my sounding board for all ideas and a wonderfully talented artist currently working hard for her first solo exhibition in Australia.

And I want to thank my parents whose thoughtful love in taking me to museums and zoos in the late 1950s before I ever went to primary school and when most parents would not have had the imagination to see what a small boy might really enjoy, is, as much as anything, the root of the scholarly career I have pursued with enormous pleasure pretty much every day of the last thirty-four years.

Pleasingly, this book was finished on the Feast Day of St Gerasimos the Righteous of Jordan whose holiness gave him authority over wild animals. He shared his cell with a lion which adopted a vegetarian diet and could even be trusted to look after the monastery's donkey.

John Simons
Wahroonga, New South Wales

CHAPTER ONE

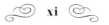

Jaguars Make Awkward Pets

One fine day in early 1881 the mist was still hanging like Spanish moss between the trees in Windsor Great Park and the deer were venturing out to graze and to display themselves in groups which owed much to the compositions of Sir Edwin Landseer. For these were cultivated deer, members of the Royal household and they knew that although they might one day furnish the tables at the great banquets of state held in the castle they had, in the meantime, to preserve the standards expected of their high position. The Great Park was, in any case, a safe place for them. The wild creatures that had occasionally prowled there in the days of George III had long been banished to the Zoological Gardens, the kangaroos that had bred there so successfully – and so recently that the oldest stags could still remember them – no longer roamed and all was peaceful domesticity. So the deer munched away without much thought to past or future and looked forward only to another day of mild weather and nothing to make them anxious or frightened. Suddenly one of them looked up. The others followed suit and before they could even comprehend the ghastly event that was about to overtake them a gorse bush seemed to catch fire or rather fire flew from a gorse bush. But it wasn't fire. It was an animal. To be exact it was a jaguar and before the deer could gather their thoughts three lay dead and gory while another was dragged away into the fiery gorse bush by the fell predator.

One fine day in early 1881 Queen Victoria was strolling on the battlements of Windsor Castle. She looked down the Chase and approved the lacy mist which sparkled between the trees like the lamps that had been lit to celebrate her marriage to Albert. She approved still more the timid decorousness of the deer which were beginning to make their way out of the trees to feed and arrange themselves solely for her pleasure. She loved the deer and her dear Albert had often remarked to her how their presence not only gave the clipped landscape of the Great Park an air of their sweet Balmoral and a premonition of their annual retreat to their beloved Highlands but also in their gentle domestication reminded everyone that through familial love nature could be tamed and even landscape itself become a model of the ideal home.

As Queen Victoria mused happily a strange thing happened. A thing so strange she initially assumed that she had, in her contented but bittersweet memorial of Albert, begun to dream. But she soon realised that this was not a dream. She saw what at first she thought was an orange dog leap from the shrubbery and grasp first one then three more of her pets by the neck, bringing them to the ground and leaving them lying still in widening pools of blood. As she watched, the dog – which she now could see was a big cat – dragged one deer off and out of sight presumably to eat it.

"John," she cried out, "John." In less than thirty seconds a huge man in full Highland dress came running and stopped a respectful distance from his monarch, his face both puzzled and anxious as he looked around for the source of her alarm. His eyes followed hers and he saw the dark patches spreading on the Chase and the still bodies of the deer now surrounded, as if they were being boiled, by the vapour which rose from the hot blood as it met the cold morning air. In that instant Brown grasped the whole matter. John Brown said nothing but grimly strode away and the Queen watched as he emerged from the Castle gates and strode angrily towards the scene of the massacre clutching a massive walking stick, his kilt swinging as he walked, like the tail of an angry tom cat.

"Dear John," thought Queen Victoria, "no thought for himself but only for me."

Although I can't be sure that the incident I have just described happened quite as I've described it – in fact, I can be pretty sure it did not – I can assure the reader that it really did happen. A jaguar really did attack and kill deer in Windsor Great Park and Queen Victoria really did send her faithful servant – some say her secret husband – John Brown to deal with the problem. We even know the name of the jaguar: he was called Affums.

Affums belonged to Lady Florence Dixie (neé Douglas) sister of the Marquess of Queensberry and therefore aunt to Lord Alfred Douglas, Oscar Wilde's beloved "Bosie". Wildness ran in the Queensberry family and Lady Florence was an enterprising soul. During her life she visited Patagonia (which is where she acquired Affums and where a hotel is still named after her), was a war correspondent in South Africa and Zululand and she organized the first English ladies' soccer tour of Scotland. She also clearly had a way with animals as when she was attacked by knife-wielding Fenians she was saved both by the trusty whalebone of her corsetry which deflected their treacherous blades and by the unexpected intervention of a St Bernard dog who just happened to be passing and who pitched in on Lady Florence's side. The invincible alliance of a whaleboned corset and a huge infuriated dog on the lookout for someone to rescue proved too much for the attackers – in later life Lady Dixie claimed they had actually kidnapped her although no one believed her; indeed, hardly anyone really believed she was attacked at all. She was that kind of woman. In spite of the wild household in which he found himself – clearly a far more eventful place than his native Patagonia – Affums appears to have been a docile and peaceful creature. Lady Florence and her husband often used to sit in his cage and chat to him of an evening although she discouraged Bosie from getting too close even when Affums was chained up.

As we have seen, Affums eventually escaped from his domestic prison but what is interesting is that after due apologies had been made to Queen Victoria and Brown had been pacified – these must have been tricky conversations – Affums was not destroyed as he certainly would be today. He was sent to the zoo. But given that Lady Dixie spent much of her time in Patagonia hunting what passes for big game there, Affums was lucky to end up in the zoo and at least he had the memory of that gloriously gory morning in the Great Park.

Had Lord Baden-Powell known about Affums he might not have been so keen to acquire Squirks his pet panther. Like Lady Dixie, Lord Baden-Powell loved to shoot wild animals – he also loved executions and would travel miles to see one – so Squirks was a lucky survivor and the kind of creature that many a young British officer posted to India acquired after the First War of Independence (or the Indian Mutiny as they would have called it) precluded the kind of relationships with Indian women that a previous generation of officers had enjoyed in the heyday of John Company. When Baden-Powell left India he made several attempts to find a new home for Squirks. But Squirks would have none of it and after much smashing of china and tearing of soft furnishings and bed linen he was always returned with thanks. So Baden-Powell sold him to Mr Jamrach about whom we shall hear a great deal later.

What these two anecdotes are intended to establish is that among a certain tier of the population there was nothing exceptional about owning an exotic animal. It may not have been common but it was by no means unusual and the increasing reach of the British Empire made it easier and easier to acquire such creatures either for yourself when you visited, like Lady Dixie and Lord Baden-Powell, or through purchase from one of the London- or Liverpool-based animal dealers. This was how the painter Dante Gabriel Rossetti acquired the menagerie he kept in the garden of his house at Cheyne Walk in Chelsea and how the great aristocratic naturalists like Lord Rothschild at Tring or Lord Stanley at Knowsley developed their massive collections.

However, it was not only the aristocratic and well to do who had the chance to enjoy exotic animals and this book starts from a very simple question which occurred to me one day while I was thinking of something else:

> If you were born in, say, Grantham in Lincolnshire in 1837 and lived until 1901 (the dates of Queen Victoria's marvel-filled reign which form the chronological brackets for this study) and never travelled more than thirty miles in any direction how likely was it that you would have seen a hippopotamus at least once before you died?

The answer, as this book will show, is highly likely. And if it wasn't a hippopotamus you saw then it would certainly have been an elephant or a lion or a North American bison.

How might this have happened? Well, you almost certainly would have been somewhere within striking distance of one of the many travelling menageries which criss-crossed the roads of England throughout the nineteenth century. Some of these were enormous with up to 2,000 animals of all varieties. You might have been to a circus although in the Victorian era circuses were largely horse-based (a travelling version of the "hippodramas" which were a spectacular fad in London and Paris) except for the odd lion-taming act or you might have been lucky enough to see Buffalo Bill's Wild West Show when it passed nearby. You might have lived near one of the great houses where the local lord kept a private menagerie – I have mentioned Tring and Knowsley but there were many others. You might have lived near a great house where the owner was an enthusiast of the accli-matisation movement and was attempting to breed and maintain a herd of exotic creatures (elands and kangaroos were popular) as a contribution to the social problem of finding protein for an increasingly urbanized and increas-ingly numerical working class. You might have known a soldier or sailor returned from Imperial duties with a parrot on the shoulder or a leopard on a lead. You might have known a comfortably off village doctor or genteel lady naturalist who kept just one or two interesting pets; a pair of budgerigars say or a tortoise. You might have caught the end of the tradition of wandering Romany bear keepers or one of the new generation of itinerant Savoyard musicians with his marmoset in a revolving cage. Depending on where you lived you might have seen the warehouse of one of the main traders in exotic creatures. You might have seen stuffed rarities displayed in the local museums which were springing up out of the philanthropic efforts of local Philosophical Societies or private benefactors. Finally, you might have met one of the odd animals who just turn up from time to time: the tiger which prowled down St George's Street East in London with a boy in its mouth, the polar bear that rampaged up Bold Street in Liverpool and killed a dog, the kangaroo which terrified the citizens of Budleigh Salterton, the panicking tapir which cleared a crowd from Rochdale town hall more efficiently than a water cannon or, indeed, Affums on his way home, bloody-mouthed, from his excursion to Windsor Great Park. All of these sites of encounter will be dealt with in more detail in subsequent chapters.

The fact is that Victorian England (and Scotland and Wales) was alive with all manner of creatures that shouldn't have been there and these were not only in the zoological gardens which the concerned and enlightened civic leaders of the big cities founded to offer an educational and cultural space for the improvement of the working population as well as the informing of the middle classes and gentry. The animals of the Americas, Australasia, India and Africa walked the lanes of England or travelled in vast mobile animal houses. They wandered the parks of the aristocracy and they lived in the corners of the ornate drawing rooms and fussy conservatories of the middle classes. And around them and between them moved the labouring poor, the domestic servants, the miners, the mill hands, the soldiers, the sailors and the hard-pressed clerks that kept the whole Imperial show on the road.

This book is, then, about exotic animals in Victorian England. But what is an exotic animal? For the purposes of this study I speak about exotic animals not solely when I mean an animal which is not indigenous to the British Isles but mainly and more commonly when I mean an animal from a distant country that has been imported into England for the purposes of education, entertainment, acclimatisation or sheer exuberance. So for the purposes of this book rabbits do not count as exotic animals. They are so much part of the English rural scene that people forget that they are not indigenous and came over with the Normans in 1066. But no one would, I think, wish to claim rabbits as exotic in the way that an escaped boa constrictor slithering around on Tunbridge Wells Common (never found as far as I can tell) or, indeed, a llama living on Lady Angela Burdett Coutts's lawn in Hampstead is exotic.

There is some awareness of the outsider nature of introduced species of course. For example, the grey squirrel is well known as a non-indigenous immigrant and most people can weave a narrative which combines ecological concern with xenophobia in equal measure around the greys' fatal assault on the native red squirrel population. The rat-like and ruthlessly efficient American interloper tears the nuts from the trees before the gentler, fluffier, Beatrix Potterised and, above all, English, red can get at them. Now the even more fearsome black squirrel is at large and this is threatening the greys in their turn. In Australia and New Zealand introduced animals – the rabbit in Australia, the possum in New Zealand, and feral cats, dogs and foxes in both – have done astonishing amounts of damage to the indigenous flora and fauna. But again, these creatures would not be seen as exotic in the way that, say, the first elephant to visit Australia was seen as exotic or even the way in which the copy of Frémiet's notorious sculpture of a gorilla making off with a naked woman was seen as exotic (among other things) when it was exhibited in Melbourne in 1897. This is partly because the dominant populations and the residual dominant culture in both of these countries are European and specifically Anglo-Celtic and so although these animals are introduced they are also familiar. The same applies to merino sheep or Charolais cattle in England. These are both introduced but it's difficult to see a farm animal as exotic. While in Australia and New Zealand, sheep, cattle, horses, deer and trout – the introduced animals that have not destroyed the eco-system (although in the first two cases they have, in fact, profoundly changed it to the point of destruction) – would rarely, if ever, be seen as exotic by the non-indige-nous human population.

So to be exotic for my purposes an animal either has to come from a long way away from the point at which it is encountered or it has to be perceived as profoundly foreign because of its distance from any of the commonly encountered animals of the region. In practice this means that it almost certainly has to come from outside of Europe – bears and marmosets only just about count in the regard – and that means India, Africa, some other part of Asia and, more rarely, Australasia and the Americas. In other words an exotic animal has really to have come from the overseas colonies and dominions of the British Empire.

There had, of course, been exotic animals in England before any thought of the massive overseas Empire that had come into being by the later nine-teenth century had begun to form in anyone's mind. Most famously perhaps there was the Tower Menagerie. This was a collection of animals kept, as the name implies, in the Tower of London. It most famously started with and always included the lions who are part of the regal arms of England – lions and the display of power go together and this can be seen from the hunting scenes on the Assyrian reliefs in the British Museum through to recent events in Libya where even when the days of the regime were clearly numbered one of the late Colonel Gaddaffi's sons made a point of visiting the lions in Tripoli Zoo. Matthew Paris records the elephant that was given to Henry III by Louis IX of France and actually drew a charming picture of it for his *Chronica Majora*. The elephant lived on an unsuitable and expensive diet of steak and red wine and died in 1257 after one magnum of claret too many. It was not the first in England however, as two war elephants came over on Julius Caesar's major raid in 44 BC and one drowned while crossing the Thames. Henry III also had a polar bear which was given to him by the King of Norway. This was kept in the Tower on a long chain so that it could pad down the Thames for a swim and I believe that polar bears may also have come back to England with Martin Frobisher and were exhibited for Elizabeth I at Hampton Court along with two Inuits in 1577. Subsequent monarchs expanded the Tower Menagerie which came to include really exotic animals such as kangaroos. In the Georgian period the Menagerie expanded to Windsor Great Park where kangaroos were successfully bred and where, on one occasion, a leopard, gift from a senior administrator in India, escaped after an unsuccessful attempt to stage a stag hunt (this was recorded in a painting by Stubbs who also painted – from its skin and skull – the first kangaroo to arrive in England). Princess Charlotte kept pet kangaroos and Princess Caroline kept parrots at what is now known as the Queen's Cottage. Bears were a common enough sight both as dancing bears on the roads with their Romany keepers and as the fighting bears in the Bear Garden on the South Bank. Contrary to popular belief the bears were not baited to death and we know the names of some of them – Sackerson, Old Harry Hunks and Tom a Lincoln for example – indeed it may even be the case that bears occasionally left the Bear Garden to perform on stage in one of the theatres (later including Shakespeare's famous Globe) that clustered on the South Bank in Elizabethan and Jacobean London's entertainment quarter. Certainly, a passage in George Peele's play *The Old Wives Tale* suggests this and what are we to make of Shakespeare's most famous stage direction, "Exit, pursued by a bear"?

However, before the nineteenth century exotic animals were a comparative rarity and certainly only available for an encounter if you lived in London or maybe Bristol or one of the important ports of the earlier period. But after the mid eighteenth century the number of exotic creatures in Britain was increased in both quantity and diversity and at an ever accelerating rate by two closely related phenomena: the rise of science and the rise of Empire.

The scientific revolution of the eighteenth century was fuelled by the Enlightenment paradigm shift by which, very broadly, an inquiring, empirical and evidential world view replaced a faith-based world view with all the intellectual and political implications that such a change entails. From the point of view of animals this meant two things. Firstly animals would come to be studied in a new way; secondly that the opening up of the known (to Europeans) world meant that animals would travel more widely than ever before. The days when an elephant trudging wearily over the Alps was seen as a miracle were long gone. This is the age when wombats will visit India and black swans will adorn the ornamental lakes of Malmaison. Both of these examples point up the role of Empire in this expansion for the wombat was a pet of Lord Wellesley the Governor General and the black swans came back with Captain Baudin's expedition to Australia and formed a key element in the Empress Joséphine's Australian garden.

Just as the furnaces of the mills and factories of the Industrial Revolution had to be fuelled by an ever-more ruthless and daring extraction of natural resources so the laboratories of the scientific revolution required an ever-more ruthless exploitation of animals. As the world expanded, the curiosity of scientists – mainly gentlemen of leisure although some, like Sir Joseph Banks and his entourage and, of course, Charles Darwin, were serious explorers in their own right – turned towards the reports of the many new species that were being discovered and could only be satisfied by samples of the creatures themselves. At first these were mainly dead but, increasingly, animals arrived alive even from as far away as New Zealand and although they didn't always survive long this was the beginning of the exotic explosion of the Victorian era. Of course, it was not only scientists who participated in the benefits of these new discoveries. New lands enabled new products and industries and these could be based on exotic animals. Most people will know about the assault on the Canadian beaver and seal carried out by the Hudson's Bay Company to feed the desire for felts and furs and also the development of the trade in bear skins – which still continues today in the supply of ceremonial hats to the Brigade of Guards. Less well known are the trades in koala and wombat skins from Australia.

Under these pressures some species became extinct or were pushed to the edge of extinction. Although habitat loss is the prime factor in the decline of koala numbers today the massive culls – in 1889 alone 300,000 koalas were killed for their skins – of the late nineteenth and early twentieth century must have taken their toll on species viability. Of course, we all know about the dodo and although this had been extinct after over-exploitation for food by the crews of European ships visiting its home on Mauritius for nearly 200 years it made several reappearances in Victorian England as scientists attempted, with various degrees of success and credibility, to reconstruct it and also as a star player in the works of Lewis Carroll. Sometimes it was science itself that caused the damage. The relative scarcity of the duckbilled platypus and echidna today is almost certainly the result of the massive trapping that was carried out as well-meaning scientists attempted to uncover the mysterious secrets of monotreme reproduction.

But the main effect of all of these things was that exotic animals began to pour into England and as the Empire expanded and consolidated, the trickle became a flood. The early explorers were abducting relatively small numbers from uncolonised lands where they had to provide their own security against local populations who often viewed them with various degrees of hostility. But the safety provided by a full colonial administration backed up by the Royal Navy, a regiment of foot, a couple of squadrons of cavalry and a battery of artillery meant that more extensive commercial ventures were increasingly possible and the profession of commercial trader in live exotic animals came into being. In addition, there was a growth in travel from England to the Colonies and back and some of the early ships returning from Australia, for example, were described as being like Noah's ark. They were stuffed with kangaroos, emus, cockatoos and parrots of every description. When the great Governor of New South Wales, Lachlan Macquarie returned to Scotland in 1822 his ship, the *Surrey*, was freighted with his personal menagerie of seven kangaroos, six emus, seven black swans, four Cape Barren geese, one Narang emu, two white cockatoos, two bronze-wing pigeons, four Wanga-Wanga pigeons, and a range of parrots or lorikeets. There were also two Aborigines. Pretty much everything was dead, including one of the Aborigines, by the time they got to Deptford. In addition, Macquarie had a large collection of native plants and a chest containing the stuffed or preserved remains of seventy-six birds, thirty-two butterflies, nearly 300 beetles and other insects as well as numerous sea shells, plant specimens and botanical and ethnographic curiosities. Macquarie's collection was not untypical for a gentleman of his type and age but many more humble individuals made the long voyage home with just one or two creatures. Of course, once back in England these animals seemed less attractive than they had done in Sydney Cove so they found their way to the animal traders in much the same way that raffia donkeys from the Costa Brava found their way to charity shops in the 1980s.

But if it was just a question of an unwanted souvenir or the subject of a temporary or even sustained scientific interest there would not, I think, be a sufficient explanation for the phenomenon which this book seeks to describe.

A more sophisticated account of the issue must look to the role of Empire itself. Not only in the way that Empire shaped scientific and economic views of the natural world, but also in the way it shaped the consciousness of its citizens. Post-colonial theory is the branch of academic study which explores this as it affected the subjects of the Empire (that is the colonised peoples). What I wish to show here is how Empire shaped the world view of its governing peoples even if those people were born in Grantham Lincolnshire and never travelled more than thirty miles in any direction all their life.

Before I do this I want to draw an exclusion zone around one aspect of this topic and that is the taking to England (and other European countries) of indigenous peoples for display and study. I have already mentioned Frobisher's Inuits and the indigenous Australians who returned with Macquarie (although these were familiar and trusted companions and not anthropological specimens). The Tahitian Omai was a well-known face in Georgian London and samples of his visiting card – he styled himself "Mr Omai" – still survive. But by the later nineteenth century, shows featuring exotic peoples were common across Europe sometimes as pure entertainment and sometimes as the site of what was genuinely meant to be anthropological study. In London, for example, you could – between 1830 and 1860 – have seen various groups of Native Americans, Inuits, indigenous Australians, Torres Strait islanders, Khoisan (bushmen), Cook islanders, a Barbadian with albinism and a Chinese lady with bound feet. The idea of "native villages" became popular, perhaps the most famous one being the Japanese village which was set up at Humphrys' Hall in Knightsbridge between 1885 and 1887 and gave Gilbert and Sullivan the idea for the *Mikado* as well as stimulating the vogue for *Japonaiserie* in interior design, art and fashion. When the indigenous Australian cricket team visited England in 1864 the breaks between innings were enlivened by various displays of native skills such as boomerang throwing and so influential was this event that when the first "official" Australian team visited in 1877 one puzzled citizen of Empire is recorded as having voiced his bemusement from the crowd with a cry of "Why! They ain't black!" I have already mentioned Buffalo Bill's Wild West Show which is another example of this kind of display. People from the Colonies were also studied in anthropological museums and zoological gardens occasionally included displays of First People. Occasionally this process happened in reverse as in the case of the British sailors who found themselves shipwrecked in 1827 and made their way back on foot across China to the British settlement at Canton – they arrived in 1828 – keeping body and soul together by charging people to look at them. For indigenous Australians this has been a particularly distressing history for two reasons: firstly, it was not until 1967 that Australian law recognized them as not being part of the local flora and fauna and so they feel especially sensitive to anything that puts them on a par with animals or scientific specimens (as, I imagine, would you or I); secondly, the human remains kept in various European and American museums are very dear to them and they have campaigned hard but with mixed success for their return to Australia where they can be properly buried and their spirits properly attended to. And this should be done immediately – the bones of ancestors should not be treated like the Elgin marbles.

So although looking at the issue from a purely Victorian perspective it might be correct to include the collection and display – whether for entertainment or ethnographic research – of native peoples under the category of the collection and display of exotic animals I am taking the view that this topic is the subject of an entirely different book and it will not be further addressed in the current work except tangentially in the treatment of shows and circuses in a later chapter.

Nevertheless, understanding this phenomenon is important to understanding the broader points about the Imperial world view that I now wish to make. If you are a citizen of the dominant culture of a massive Empire which is, apparently, capable of more or less unlimited expansion, you feel a certain superiority even if your station in life is a humble one. Of course, to make your station even less humble you can always go to the Colonies where however menial your job is you will always be superior to the local people. But the Imperial mentality extends far beyond people. It applies to the whole of the colonised ecosystem as well as to natural resources such as fuel and metals.

The impact of European Imperial expansion on the eco-systems of the colonies is far less studied than the impact on the peoples and the impact of the Islamic Imperial expansion on the plants and animals of Europe and Africa has not, to the best of my knowledge, been studied at all in spite of the fact that this expansion had greater longevity than that of the European empires and is still in place to a greater degree than anything imposed by Europeans. Gerôme's magnificent Orientalist painting *The Pasha's Sorrow*, which shows an Arab dignitary in melancholy contemplation of the body of his dead pet tiger laid out on a beautiful carpet strewn with rose petals, is a very rare example of this. It also has the added complexity of being a work in a western imperialist genre (Orientalism) which depicts the impact of non-western imperialism. The underlying problem here is that imperialism is seen as a specifically European phenomenon which, of course, it is not: by far the most successful post-Medieval Empire was the Ottoman Empire which ruled large chunks of Europe, North Africa and the Middle East for over 500 years. The British Empire was a temporary phenomenon compared with what the Turks achieved.

So when the British arrived in a new colony they not only set about organizing the people, they also considered the ecosystem. This consideration took several forms. Firstly, it involved the inventory of the natural resources available, sometimes but by no means always, using the advice of the local people. Secondly, it almost always involved trying to establish the plants and animals that were familiar to British tastes or which were required for the economic success of the particular colonial venture. In Australia, for example, a great deal of the first colonists' time was expended on trying to establish flax from which to make sails to go with the masts they hoped to construct from the tall and ramrod-straight Norfolk Island pines. This was not a success as flax doesn't do well in Australia and although Norfolk Island pines look as if they were made for mast-building they are not, in fact, very suited to this use.

Similarly, when the First Fleet arrived in Australia they found that corn (maize) grew well but eventually this crop was largely abandoned for the more familiar wheat which doesn't thrive as well as corn. There were also attempts in various colonies to make the landscape more English. Foxes and rabbits were soon introduced to provide sport and food and soon set about their work of devastating local animals and plants. Song birds were introduced into both Australia and New Zealand for no other purpose than to recreate an English soundscape. Then there was acclimatisation which I will deal with in slightly more detail below. Thirdly, there was an inventory of wildlife to decide what could be farmed, eaten or used as pack or draught animals, what could be hunted and what simply required extermination. By the later nineteenth century a combination of Darwinism and a kind of deterministic muscular Christianity could have a fatal impact on some species if observation could not determine that species' place in either the evolutionary chain or the divine plan. Hunting, especially big game hunting, became one of the most notable manifestations of Imperial domination and the old Africa hand with his zebra skins or the old India hand with his tiger skins became a familiar figure both at home and abroad.

In other words, an Imperial system requires the total domination of the colonised environment and this mentality was shared across the great majority of the colonising people even if they never stirred beyond thirty miles of Grantham. So when exotic animals passed nearby, what was on display were not simply the wonders of nature but, perhaps more importantly and often quite explicitly, the spoils of Empire. The Romans had understood this only too well and their mighty depredation of African animals in particular led to the extinction of the North African elephant and the genetic weakening of the now probably extinct Barbary lions. Their displays of captured animals in Triumph processions as well as the great beast shows in the Colosseum and at amphitheatres all over the Roman world were precisely conceived to demonstrate the superiority of their civilisation over all others (although they were always worried about the Greeks). The classically trained ideologues and officers of the British Empire knew this history as well as, if not better than, they knew their own and were concerned that in their own Imperial project the best features of Rome might be reproduced. For them this meant culture, civilisation and the rule of law but these worthy concepts were benefits for the colonised people and they did not necessarily extend to the colonised animals.

Big game hunting was, however, only a small part of the picture, albeit the most spectacular part. More important was the display of the spoils of Empire in the home country and this is where the zoos, menageries and animal shows that are the subject of this book came in. The slow progress of the caravans of, say, Bostock's travelling menagerie along the high roads of England is, in this sense, the faint echo of the triumphs of ancient Rome with their cages of snarling lions, trumpeting elephants and bemused giraffes.

BOSTOCK'S MENAGERIE ON THE ROAD C. 1912

Except where the citizens of Rome turned out to cheer and throw flowers, Bostock's collection would have mainly been viewed by curious plough boys and the odd country vicar. This is the shift between the ancient world and the modern world in its most debased form and here the glorious cruelty of Rome's triumph over barbarism is replaced by an industrial and commercial venture in which cruelty is downplayed to neglect and naked suprematism becomes attendance at a sideshow. As Karl Marx said, history repeats itself, the first time as tragedy, the second time as farce.

So the encounters with exotic animals that I am going to trace all over England should be read not only as encounters with a strangeness and difference but also as a reinforcement of a single mental picture and a set of values which set the world in a hierarchy which was signified by the fact that you could come face to face with a tiger in the middle of prime English farm land. But the key thing is that the tiger was caged.

An aspect of the Imperial project as it applied to animals and which brings together many of the disparate themes sketched out in this introduction, was acclimatisation. Acclimatisation was not only a British pursuit. The French were, if anything, even more keen on it with the Parisian *Jardin d'Acclimatation* forming a specialised zoo quite different from other kinds and watched over for many years by the eminent naturalist Geoffroy de St Hilaire. Judging from the records of the relative longevity of animals in French as opposed to British acclimatisation collections the French were also more successful at it. The whole acclimatisation project achieved very little in the sense that few useful animals were actually successfully introduced into Europe. The flow the other way was very different with all manner of agricultural animals and useful fish being transplanted into the colonies. Acclimatisation was not confined to the British and French though. The Russians tried it via the Imperial Russian Conservation Society and there were various acclimatisation societies in the United States and the Hawaiian Islands. Other countries or colonies which had societies included Algeria, Ceylon, China, Egypt, Holland, India, Italy, Portugal (Madeira), Prussia, Sicily, South Africa, Spain, and Switzerland. In addition there were vigorous conservation societies in the Australian states (still essentially independent colonies pre-Federation in 1900) and scattered all over New Zealand. Indeed, Sir George Grey in New Zealand was an astonishingly active advocate of acclimatisation and introduced, among other species, kangaroos, wallabies, monkeys, zebras, kookaburras, peacocks, antelopes and deer to Kawau Island. New Zealand has no indigenous mammals and so all such animals there are in some sense acclimatised. A flavour of the enthusiasm for acclimatisation can be had from the founder of the Acclimatisation Society of Victoria, Edward Wilson. "If it lives", said Wilson, "we want it". The Society populated the colony's air with starlings and sparrows and its rivers with carp and started Melbourne Zoo originally as a holding pen for its various imports. A medal awarded by the Society in 1868 shows a rabbit, a hare, an alpaca, an ostrich, a goat, a (white) swan, and a pheasant as well as a small bird (presumably a sparrow or starling) in flight. Not all of these importations were happy.

In Britain acclimatisation had one key purpose and that was to find and acclimatise exotic species that could be successfully farmed in order to increase the efficiency of meat farming and therefore the quantity of affordable and good quality protein to feed the growing population and especially the cities. There was a secondary motivation among some of the gentry which was to stock their parks with interesting exotic animals but the economic and agricultural impulse was by far the most important driver. Attempts were made to interest people in eating horse meat as well but as Frank Buckland – of whom much more below – admitted, even calling it "hippocrene" was a poor inducement to persuade the English to take up this suspiciously Gallic taste.

The Acclimatisation Society of the United Kingdom was founded in 1860 with a separate branch being founded in Guernsey in 1864. This followed the famous "eland dinner" which was organised by Sir Richard Owen and attended by an enthusiastic Frank Buckland. At this dinner, which was held on 19th January 1860 (Buckland later misremembered it as having taken place on the 22nd) at the Aldersgate tavern in London, the influential guests were served with pike, American partridges, and wild goose. But the main point of the dinner was the roast eland. Sir Richard Owen then gave a lecture on the idea of acclimatisation and, especially the potential of eland. As he subsequently wrote:

> It is not too much to expect that in twenty years eland venison will be at least an attainable article of food and seeing the rapidity with which it arrives at maturity, its weight, and its capacity for feeding, it is quite possible that before the expiration of the century it may be removed from the category of animals of luxury to the more solid and useful list of the farm.

This is as clear an exposition of the basic principles and motivations of acclimatisation as one could wish for and, immediately following the formation of the Society, several of its wealthy and influential founding members set up experiments in eland farming. The Earl of Derby had already experimented with this animal at Knowsley and now Viscount Hill, the Marquess of Breadalbane and Lord Egerton tried their luck. Lord Powerscourt was experimenting with hybrids of exotic and native deer in Ireland although these did not breed well and his hybrids of Chinese sheep produced such inferior meat that local butchers wouldn't touch it. It was also discovered that elands couldn't thrive in the misty moistness of the green meadows of County Wicklow and so Lord Powerscourt's herd was given to King Victor Emmanuel of Italy and Sardinia.

But among the founders of the Acclimatisation Society none was more influential or, indeed, more interesting, than Frank Buckland. Buckland was the son of the notable pioneering paleontologist William Buckland, the Dean of Christchurch. One could while away a long evening and more with anecdotes about William and Frank Buckland and I do not want to repeat what I have written elsewhere in my book *Rossetti's Wombat* but suffice to say they were both fascinated by the idea of extending the range of edible animals and in their different ways set about the gastronomic conquest of the entire animal kingdom. Frank's first experiments with such delights as porpoise (although he made amends to a living porpoise later in his life by pouring a bottle of brandy down its neck when it was sickening – surprisingly the animal revived) when he was at Oxford seem like juvenilia when compared with his mature exploits. Among other things he sampled a leopard which had been dead and buried three days. When the eland dinner invitation dropped through the letter box Frank must have been beside himself with excitement. Within a very short time he had produced the following list as excellent prospects for acclimatisaton alongside the eland: the oryx, the wildebeest, the kudu, the wapiti, the barasingha, the sambar, the chital, the Virginia deer, the moose and the elk, the bison, the nilgai, the yak, the beaver, the wallaby, guanaco, the llama, the alpaca and the vicuña. He also had a pretty good list of birds and fish.

By July 1862 Buckland was able to record an enormously varied dinner held by the Society and including a massive variety of exotic foodstuffs which included trepang, bird's nest soup, sea weed and kangaroo. In this age of gastronomic variety and especially of familiarity with Chinese and Japanese cuisines it is perhaps hard to appreciate just how exotic some of the items on this menu actually must have seemed. It is clear also that although much of the menu included samples from animals which were good candidates for acclimatisation other dishes were there simply to satisfy the gustatory curiosity of the somewhat eccentric group which formed itself around the acclimatisation project.

Acclimatisation offers an easy way to understand what was happening when exotic animals made their way to Victorian England. It was, however, a somewhat specialised project and one which had a very clear focus, programme and function. Nevertheless this clarity helps to expose how the presence of exotic animals was underpinned by and was an underpinning of the broader Imperial project as it impacted on the cultural sphere more generally and on the formation of national identities. It is now time to turn to more varied and complex examples. And to some good stories.

The Trade in Exotic Animals

The Tiger that Swallowed the Boy or Snakes (by the Mile)

If you had been wandering in the East End of London on 6th January 1839 and, more precisely, meandering down Ratcliffe Highway towards Katherine Dock you would have seen a number of things. The normal street traders were beginning to set up their shops and stalls. Some were already hanging out their wares. You might have seen the prostitutes for which the area was notorious blearily plying their way home to get some day-time sleep, the bright dresses and shawls that signified their trade a splash of colour in the dull red street although in the brightening morning they look bedraggled like parrots that have been caught out in the monsoon. You might have seen the landlord of the Prince Regent tavern sweeping away the debris of the night before; the broken glass perhaps and swilling down the street to flush away the blood of a sailor whose night ashore has ended badly. You might have seen any or all of these things but you would certainly have seen a Bengal tiger padding angrily along dragging the remains of a half-eaten dog and followed at a respectful distance by a small crowd.

If you had been wandering in the East End of London on 26th October 1857 and, more precisely, meandering down St George Street east (it had once been called Ratcliffe Highway but this name had been abandoned to try to expunge – perhaps to exorcise – the memory of the notorious Ratcliffe Highway murders, the alleged perpetrator of which still lies, with his eyes wide open in the dark, in a suicide's grave somewhere between New Street and Cannon Street) towards St Katherine Docks you would have seen a number of things. The normal street traders were beginning to set up their shops and stalls. Some were already hanging out their wares. You might have seen the prostitutes for which the area was notorious blearily plying their way home to get some day time sleep, the bright dresses and shawls that signified their trade a splash of colour in the dull red street although in the brightening morning they look bedraggled like parrots that have been caught out in the monsoon. You might have seen the landlord of the Prince Regent tavern sweeping away the debris of the night before; the broken glass perhaps and swilling down the street to flush away the blood of a sailor whose night ashore has ended badly. You might have seen any or all of these things but you would certainly have seen a Bengal tiger padding angrily along with a boy in its mouth and a man shouting for a crowbar.

Curiously the area was known as Tiger Bay not for the proliferation of tigers but for the ferocity of its prostitutes. In 1873, *Routledge's Popular Guide to London* characterised it as:

> ...remarkable for nothing if not its numerous marine store shops,, gin shops, and slop shops, its fish stalls in the streets, and its scores of unbonneted women.

As the old sea shanty, perhaps one known to Captain James Cook who lived here for a while, goes:

> Oh me riggin's slack, Aye, me rattlin's are fray'd,
>
> I've rattled my riggin' down Ratcliffe Highway!

In 1839 Wombwell's famous travelling menagerie was resting nearby and the tiger had made off in the night. In addition to eating the dog it savaged, although not fatally, anyone who dared to come near it and was eventually cornered in a backyard and contained until the menagerie staff arrived and were able to recapture it.

In 1857 a tiger was being transported as part of a van-load of wild animals which had arrived, by ship, in London only the day before. While a cage full of leopards was being unloaded in a yard in Betts Street the tiger put his front paws against the bars at the front of his cage and his back against the all too flimsy planking along the back and by pushing with all his might and main broke through and pounced down into the street, scattering the crowd that had gathered to watch the curious proceedings. As the tiger strolled away

WOMBWELL'S MENAGERIE ON THE ROAD C. 1856

young John Wade, who was just turned nine (although he looks younger as the indifferent food that he has endured all his life has made him small for his age), was delighted by the magnificent spectacle and reached out to stroke him with disastrous consequences. The tiger is angry. He is still seasick. He is stiff from his long confinement in a travelling crate. He is hungry from the poor diet he has had to endure on his long journey from India. He is confused by the hubbub around him.

The tiger – and, indeed, the whole consignment of dangerous creatures landed that day – belonged to Charles Jamrach, born at Memel in 1815 Johann Christian Carl Jamrach, dealer in wild beasts from his shop at 179–180 St George Street East and the most famous and internationally patronised provider of exotic animals in England, if not Europe. Jamrach is by now hanging on to the tiger's neck and he will now take up the story:

> My men had been seized with the same panic as the bystanders, but now I discovered one lurking round a corner, so I shouted to him to come with a crowbar; he fetched one and hit the tiger three tremendous blows over the eyes.

It was only now he released the boy. His jaws opened and his tongue protruded about seven inches. I thought the brute was dead or dying, and let go of him, but no sooner had I done so than he jumped up again. In the same moment I seized the crowbar myself and gave him, with all the strength I had left, a blow over the head. He seemed to be quite cowed, and turning tail, went back towards the stables, which fortunately were open. I drove him into the yard and, and closed the doors at once. Looking round for my tiger, I found that he had sneaked into a large empty den that stood open at the bottom of the yard. Two of my men who had jumped onto an elephant's box, now descended and pushed down the iron-barred siding of the door; and so my tiger was safe again under lock and key.

Jamrach's account, entitled "My Struggle with a Tiger" was published in the *Boy's Own Paper* in February 1879 and was accompanied by a thrilling engraving showing Jamrach grimly wrestling the crazed beast, the boy hanging limply in its mouth and the figure of Jamrach's man hastening up with the crowbar.

THE TIGER THAT SWALLOWED THE BOY, 1879

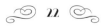

To the Rescue.

However, the fight with the tiger was not the end of the incident. In Jamrach's view the hospital to which the boy was taken had pronounced him shaken but essentially unhurt – and it is true that the *Daily News* reported on young John's positive progress only four days later – so he offered John's father £50 in compensation for this terrifying experience. But Mr Wade would have none of it and sued Jamrach for damages. He was awarded £300 of which all but sixty was swallowed up by his lawyers. Jamrach had appointed two lawyers himself but one didn't show up and the other charged his fee even though the case had been badly lost. The only compensation that Jamrach could derive from the whole sorry tale was the judge's view that instead of being punished Jamrach ought to have been rewarded for his bravery. Nevertheless, the judge felt that Jamrach was responsible and hence the damages which in the judge's view were set as low as possible. The case was held on 5th February 1858 some five months after the outrage. Although John was unhurt he did suffer lasting psychological consequences manifesting themselves in nightmares about tigers and the habit of biting his brother. Jamrach's obituary in *The Times* some 43 years later mentioned this incident and the "heavy damages" Jamrach had had to pay.

Jamrach actually had one other consolation: he sold the animal, which must have looked somewhat battered by this time, immediately to Wombwell's menagerie (the proprietors of which clearly had a penchant for errant tigers) for the £300 – this is Jamrach's figure although other accounts specify £200 or £400 – that he had had to shell out to the Wade family and their voracious counsel. Wombwell exhibited the beast as "The Tiger that Swallowed the Boy" or in some accounts "The Tiger that Swallowed the Child" and it became one of the sights of his menagerie. Its attractiveness was presumably increased when he broke out again but this time the target of his wrath was a harmless old lion who lived in the cage next door. The lion got a terrible mauling and was saved only by the thickness of his mane.

The shocking events involving the tiger made national headlines and the story was reported by most of the English and Scottish provincial newspapers. It was even reported in Welsh in *Y Baner Cymru*. However, in 1857 the minds of the English were very much set on Bengal tigers as they had watched in horror as the previously loyal sepoys of the East India Company's Bengal army rose up against British rule and were subsequently joined by units from other parts of India. They killed their officers and also massacred British civilians. The public were already jumpy about the dangers of the

Tipu's Tiger

tiger-India connection as they were familiar with the clockwork toy that had been looted from Tipu Sultan's Seringapatam palace in 1799 and which showed a more or less life-sized tiger mauling a figure who looks suspiciously like a British soldier, complete with ghastly groans from the soldier and fierce growls from the tiger. This was in the East India Company's collection and can now be seen in the Victoria and Albert museum. It was so notorious that a Staffordshire figure was made of it.

In August 1857 *Punch* had published a cartoon by Sir John Tenniel, entitled the "The British Lion's Vengeance on the Bengal Tiger" and showing a lion leaping onto a tiger which is straddling a white woman and her child. *Punch* reported gleefully on the Jamrach incident but *The Examiner* of 31ˢᵗ October published a piece entitled "A Poor Dear Tiger". In this the newspaper facetiously chastised Jamrach for being more careful of the tiger than the boy and making the point that government policy was paying too much attention to the rights and wrongs of the sepoys' case and the rights and wrongs of the Imperial presence in India and not enough to the business of protecting the British population and planning the military defeat and punishment of the rebels. So although the tiger incident seems like a curious byway of the East London scene in the middle of the nineteenth century its timing meant that it was propelled to the heart of political debate about the Empire, the morality of imposing British domination on subject peoples and the difficult matter of bringing a well-trained army back to heel. One young officer facing an army of mutineers was amazed to find how well their discipline held under fire and how they came on in good order with their flags flying and their bands playing exactly as they had been trained to do by their British superiors. It was not imagined that once the sepoys were left to their own devices and had to be commanded by native officers they would constitute any significant military force. The Duke of Wellington, once contemptuously dismissed by Napoleon as a mere "sepoy general", could have told them different.

The presence of a Bengal tiger, the very symbol of India and, now, of rebellious India in the deepest heart and home of the Empire is, at one level a statement of the potency of that Empire and its capacity to subjugate and rule its peoples no matter how far away they might be. However, once that tiger escapes it becomes a symbol of something very different especially when it picks up a white child. Jamrach may have beat it back into submission and the court may have followed the banal due process of a claim for damages case but in 1857 it is clear that a tiger was not just a tiger (as if a tiger is ever just a tiger) and in reading this episode and the contemporary response to it we can see very clearly just how significant and just how sensitive the presence of exotic animals in Victorian England could become. Jamrach may have thought he was heroically rescuing John Wade and indeed he was. But he was also fighting, whether he knew it or not, for the honour of the Empire. The blows of his crowbar on the poor dear tiger's head were the prefiguring of the crack of the gallows' platforms as they turned over, hurtling captured mutineers into their final drop or the reports of the cannons which blasted through the bodies of the mutineers strapped to their muzzles while bewhiskered ranks of British soldiers looked on impassively. Jamrach's tiger is recorded in a somewhat bizarre statue in a defunct shopping centre in Tobacco Dock.

But this was not Jamrach's first court appearance. Only the year before he had successfully sued the circus entrepreneur "Lord" George Sanger (who will feature in a later chapter) for the value of an elephant that had been delivered to him but which had died probably of internal parasites. The judge found the whole case immensely amusing and thanked both Jamrach and Sanger for the information they had provided which included the fact that elephants lived on boiled rice and treacle with a couple of biscuits as a Sunday treat.

Charles Jamrach was an extraordinary man by any account. Anyone who keeps elephants in boxes must be classed as extraordinary. The dealership he maintained in St George's Street East had not been established by him. It was a family business and he, in turn, passed it on to his sons. Jamrach's father Jacob Gerhard Gotthold Jamrach had worked as harbour master and chief of the Hamburg River Police and had noticed just how many wild animals and other exotic curiosities passed through the port. So he started buying and selling them and eventually set up a paying attraction called Handel's Menagerie at 19 Spielbudenplatz in the St Pauli area.

When the family firm relocated to London (there are persistent comments about a branch in Liverpool too but I have been unable to find any evidence of this) the menagerie was sold off to Claus Gottfried Carl Hagenbeck the father of Carl Hagenbeck, a kind of German P. T. Barnum, who would be Jamrach's only real rival in the worldwide trade in animals but who branched out into full scale zoological and ethnographic entertainments and whose legacy still exists in the form of Hamburg Zoo. *Vater* Hagenbeck was a fishmonger by trade and made sure of the freshness of his stock by employing his own fishing fleet. He was especially involved in the valuable caviar trade and in 1848 one of his teams of sturgeon fishers came back with six seals that had got entangled in their nets. Rather than killing them Hagenbeck put them in two big basins and charged people to see them. He then took them on the road and exhibited them as far afield as Berlin where he finally sold them on. This was, of course, in the midst of the 1848 risings and it is pleasing to think that while the barricades flew up and troops fired into the crowds, just around the corner people were indulging in the much more sensible and certainly safer pastime of looking at six seals in a wooden tub. This success spurred the elder Hagenbeck to buy and exhibit other animals and to set up a menagerie to rival Jamrach's. He finally bought the Jamrach Hamburg operation in 1863 (when Gotthold died) by which time the Jamrach business was already well established and thriving in a similar area of London. An image of Hagenbeck's yard by Heinrich Leutemann was published in the magazine *Daheim* in 1866. In a central position sits a seal in a wooden tub but there is also a monkey, a polar bear (in a terrifyingly small cage), a peccary, various exotic birds, a reindeer, and an indistinct stripey animal which might be a tiger cub. Carl Hagenbeck took the business to new heights and was, in the early stages, reliant on trips to London to source his animals. His brother-in law, Charles Rice, was his agent in London. Rice died young in 1879 (he was thirty-eight) but was thought of as an important figure in the animal dealing world, not least because he also covered the American market. He and Jamrach appear to have enjoyed cordial relations.

Hagenbeck later wrote that his business was greatly enhanced when the German Empire was established as a worldwide force and this again shows just how inter-related are the two phenomena of the exotic animal trade and the growth of the European Imperial project.

Meanwhile, In London, Charles Jamrach was busily building a fortune and a reputation. We may assume, from his own account of the fight with the tiger, that his Betts Street yard would have looked not unlike Hagenbeck's Hamburg establishment and, as this had been built up by the Jamrach family, it is safe to assume that they would have replicated the model when they came to London. His shop was crammed full of all manner of creatures, especially birds and was one of the sights of London. An American tourist wrote up her visit to Jamrach's for an 1877 issue of *Harper's New Monthly Magazine* and spoke of the grim atmosphere that prevailed there, of the thousands of birds packed into a room where there was a "death-like stillness" where "not one little heart was cheery enough to chirp".

The flavour of Jamrach's shop is perhaps best captured in the naturalist's Elizabeth Brightwen's description of "A Visit to Jamrach" in her 1898 book *Wild Nature Won by Kindness*. Brightwen had a varied collection of animals

JAMRACH'S SHOP

and in such books as *Inmates of My House and Garden*, *More on Wild Nature*, *Quiet Hours with Nature*, and *Last Hours with Nature*, she documents fifty-two different creatures that had, at some point, been her pets. These included animals from the English countryside as well as more exotic animals such as the lemurs Tommy, Perlie, Spectre and Phantom, Cheops the scarab beetle and Sancho the Second, an Italian toad. Elizabeth, like Jamrach, was only able to collect some of her animals because she had friends and relations throughout the Empire and these would ship her the odd curiosity.

However she also bought from Jamrach and in her account she writes first of the journey through the "labyrinth of narrow, dirty streets" and the arrival in the cacophony of Jamrach's emporium. She noticed "a fine, healthy toucan, with his marvelous bill, looking sadly out of place in a small cage in such a dingy place." "Did he ever," she asked herself, "think of his tropical forest home ... and imagine himself in happier surroundings?" Like the American author of the *Harper's New Monthly* article she was touched by the plight of the "rows and rows of Grass Parakeets: many hundreds must have been on those perches, one behind the other, poor little patient birdies, sitting in solemn silence, never moving an inch, for they were wedged in as closely as they could sit and how they could eat and live seemed a mystery." But Elizabeth had come to look at small mammals and Jamrach obliged. He started with some armadillos "very curious, but somehow not attractive as pets" thought Elizabeth and she was not tempted to buy them even when Jamrach explained that "if I got tired of it as a pet I could have it cooked, as they were excellent eating." They then moved into what I assume was the yard in Betts Street where they saw hyenas and wolves, deer and monkeys and Elizabeth's friend's hat would have been eaten by a camel if Jamrach had not warned her to dodge. They climbed a ladder to look at a Japanese cat, a monkey and a kangaroo rat which Jamrach pulled from his cage by the tail but Elizabeth found him "too large and formidable to be pleasant". Her eyes then alighted on some Peruvian guinea pigs:

> Wonderful little creatures! With hair three or four inches long, white, yellow and black, set on anyhow, sticking out in odd tufts, one side of their heads white, the other black, their eyes just like boot buttons, they were captivating; and a pair had to be chosen forthwith and packed in a basket with a tortoise and huge Egyptian lizard, and with these spoils I was not sorry to leave this place of varied noise and smells.

She called the guinea pigs Fluff and Jamrach and although they started off well enough they eventually fought and Jamrach was sent to the stable while Fluff lived in the dining room. They got on well enough outside although Elizabeth worried about a weasel who seemed to take a more than casual interest in them. Fluff was a disappointment and clearly retreated into a deep depression unrelieved by the spectacle of his mistress eating her dinner. He

> led a most inactive life. I don't think he ever had more than two ideas in his little brain – he just lived to eat and sleep, and was about as interesting as a stuffed animal would have been.

Elizabeth's account confirms a number of things about Jamrach's shop. First of all it was no fun to be there if you were an animal. Secondly, although the animals represented a very significant investment of time and money and were Jamrach's livelihood, the neglect that was apparent to visitors must have represented what, at the time, was a moderately high standard of attention to welfare and diet. Certainly, Jamrach was a more than amateur naturalist – he was, as well as being a dealer in animals a dealer in exotic sea shells and had a high reputation in the field of conchology. In fact, there is a rare snail, *Amoria jamrachi*, which was named for Jamrach by the British Museum after he had donated a specimen of the shell. In Henry Mayhew's *London Labour and the London Poor*, the trade of street sea shell seller is described and Jamrach himself was interviewed as an authority on the business. A Hamburg Trade Directory for 1847 gives his father's occupation as trader in shells and other natural items so this was clearly part of the family business from the outset.

Finally, notice the contrast between Jamrach's approach to his animals and Elizabeth's somewhat winsome idea of kindness. This illustrates very well the process of gendering that we can readily observe at this time. While men were concerned with the business of domination – and Jamrach's approach clearly shows this – the development of what we would now call a women's movement had as one of its features a new and more nurturing approach to nature and animals. In the later nineteenth century we begin to see explicit connections between various manifestations of feminism – the women's suffrage campaign, the agitation around the Married Women's Property Act, rational dress, access to higher education – and the growth of animal welfare movements. Women held protests against such things as the live export of animals to continental Europe, hunting, the trade in fur and feathers for the fashion industry and vivisection.

This gendered dichotomy is perhaps best illustrated by the passage in which Elizabeth describes her purchase of the lizard and its subsequent life with her:

> The lizard was about fourteen inches long, a really grand creature. He came from the ruins of ancient Egypt, and looked in his calm stateliness as though he might have gazed upon the Pharaohs themselves. When placed in the sun for a time he would sometimes deign to move a few inches, his massive, grey, scaly body looking very like a young crocodile. I was greatly teased about my fondness for "Rameses," as I called this new and majestic pet; there was a great fascination about him, and as I really wished to know more of his ways and habits, I carried the basket in which he lived everywhere with me indoors and out, and studied all possible ways of feeding him; but alas! Nothing would induce him to eat. After gazing for five minutes at the most tempting mealworm, he would at last raise up his mighty head and appear to be revolving great ideas to which mealworms and all sublunary things must give place. Jamrach told me that the lizard would drink milk, and once he did drink a few drops, but generally he walked into and over the saucer as if it did not exist.
>
> I believe the poor creature had been without food so long that it had lost the power of taking nourishment, and to my great regret it grew weaker and thinner, and at last it died, and all I could do was send the remains to a naturalist to be preserved somewhat after the fashion of its great namesake.

The short, sad life of Rameses – although he must have survived the voyage to England – illustrates the difference in attitudes. Elizabeth is seeking some affinity with the exotic here. She has an Egyptomaniac's desire to locate her pet in some mystical and spiritualised realm of ancient wisdom. She wants to learn about the animal and, it seems, learn from it. For her Rameses is a fragment of another great Imperial past to be cherished and studied. For Jamrach the lizard is a commodity, a part of the spoils of Empire to be sold and exhibited as the Romans might have sold and exhibited captive kings and queens.

If Rameses reminded Elizabeth of a crocodile she might really have seen one in Jamrach's shop. In his *Advance Australia* (1885) the Honourable Harold

Finch-Hatton recalled his two encounters with Big Ben a crocodile twenty-three feet in length. The first time they met was in Queensland; the second time was at Jamrach's shop.

One of Jamrach's neighbours was the Reverend Harry Jones whose memoir *East and West London* (1875) recalled his life as a pastor in one of the toughest areas of the city. Jones confirms Brightwen's account in that he too says that the shop contained mainly birds while the bigger creatures were kept in a yard. He mused on his good fortune to serve the only parish in England where "a parson could ring his bell and send his servant round to buy a lion." We know Jamrach's price for a lion. It was £100. So lions cost less than tigers. And if the £300 he got for the tiger that swallowed the boy seems a lot this was nothing compared to the £420 he got for a pair he shipped to the Sultan's private gardens in Constantinople. At one point he had three elephants and a black bear – "kindness guaranteed" – in stock. Elephants cost £400 each and such was the scale of the operation that Mark Twain recalled a deal between Barnum and Jamrach by which Jamrach was to sell Barnum eighteen elephants for $360,000. However, as one of these elephants was Jumbo, who wasn't Jamrach's to sell, I am sceptical of this report.

In 1879 the magazine *Good Words* furnished a very detailed picture of Jamrach's shop. This piece reminds us that the St George's Street East shop was also a selling museum of curiosities – a stuffed head in the Pitt Rivers museum was bought at Jamrach's although in 1895 William and Albert Edward Jamrach also made a substantial donation to that establishment – and that in addition to the Betts' Street yard there was a warehouse in Old Gravel Lane. Harry Jones had noted the firm's habit of announcing new arrivals as to be found simply "at Jamrach's" and the *Good Words* piece confirms the international extent of his network specifying agencies in Liverpool, Southampton, Plymouth, Deal, Bordeaux, Marseilles, Hamburg and elsewhere. In other words wherever exotic creatures were most likely to land Jamrach had a man there to watch and buy. We also learn that although Jamrach (as Hagenbeck was later to do on a huge scale) sent out collectors to India, Africa and America he preferred to buy creatures that had been shipped to Europe for other various reasons – like Lord Baden-Powell's Squirks as we saw in the previous chapter. This is why Hagenbeck was so dependent on the English trade before the Germans had developed an Imperial trading network of their own. There is a record of Jamrach being in Australia in 1873 but, as I shall suggest later, I think that this was probably

INSIDE JAMRACH'S SHOP

his son Anton. Another of his sons, William, certainly went on buying trips to India. Jamrach was in St Petersburg in July 1882 and seems to have been involved in supplying up to 3,000 African monkeys per year to the monkey theatres which were popular in Germany and Russia at that time.

In 1869 Frank Buckland recorded an expedition which was led by the cherishably named Monsieur Lorenzo Casanova who had taken up animal catching on behalf of Hagenbeck after the failure of his dog and monkey show. This resulted in what Jamrach himself described as "the largest consignment of wild animals that ever arrived in Europe". The expedition did most of its work on the border between Egypt and what is now Ethiopia and collected thirty-two elephants, eight giraffes, twenty antelopes, sixteen buffaloes, two rhinos, one hippo, twelve hyenas, four lions, four ostriches, twelve hornbills and a miscellany of other birds. The bigger animals walked to the Red Sea, the rest were caged using iron bars which had been transported specially for the purpose. The entourage was accompanied by 300 Arabs, ninety-five camels and eighty goats which were there to provide milk for the hippo and the rhinos. After a six-week trek across the desert in which Casanova was stung by a poisonous fly and temporarily went blind, two elephants escaped and five were killed "by accident" (how could that have happened?), the animals were put on a steamer to Trieste whence they were taken to Hamburg by train. Eventually eleven elephants, five giraffes, six antelopes, one rhino, twelve hyenas, seven hornbills and four ostriches staggered from their carriages. But maybe these animals were luckier than most of those on the S.S. *Agra* which went down off Galle (Ceylon, now Sri Lanka) on 5th October 1873. This contained a large consignment for Jamrach (priced at £4,000) although the crew managed to rescue some cobras and an elephant. A tiger swam ashore but was shot three days later by the government agent.

In 1873 Jamrach's agents could be found in Singapore and had filled the yard of the Hotel de la Paix with their purchases which included four tapirs, two orangutans, a panther, an elephant, a bear and various large birds. These formed an informal zoo and could be viewed by appointment. He had two local hunters, the Fernandez brothers, scouring the Malaysian Peninsula for more animals and was planning a shipment of eight each of rhinoceri, tapirs, tigers, and panthers as well as numerous birds.

The same *Good Words* article gives a great deal of detail about Jamrach's prices and that a single cargo could raise as much as £1,000 for the master. We also learn more about the scale of the enterprise. One consignment alone consisted of 5,000 pairs of cockatoos. No wonder they had to be packed so tightly into Jamrach's cages. Jamrach was offered a lump sum of £20,000 for his museum of shells and botanical specimens as well as cases of mounted butterflies and beetles. He turned it down. Assuming this offer was made in 1870 this represents a purchasing power at the time of writing of just under one million pounds. The fact that Jamrach turned the offer down shows just how lucrative his long-term trading prospects promised to be and how important the museum was as an integrated part of his total business. All this was in spite of the significant cost of buying the animals, paying the keepers and the equally huge cost of feeding them with the big cats alone requiring eight pounds of meat per day. But the museum was a ramshackle affair spread over two floors and so congested that at any moment one was in danger of damaging the goods and, as some of the porcelain vases on sale were priced at over £200 apiece, it was a perilous place.

Here are some of the prices quoted in the 1879 article:

A Sumatran rhinoceros (currently on loan to London Zoo) £1,000

An Indian rhinoceros ("Begum" bought from British officers in Burma) not yet priced but purchased for £1,250

Zebras £100 – £150

Camels £20

Giraffes £40

Ostriches £80

Polar bears £25 (this seems cheap but perhaps it reflects the enormous difficulty entailed in keeping such a big and fierce animal alive)

Other bears £8 – £16

Leopards £20

Lions £100

Tigers £300

Black Panthers £150

Cheetahs £80

Ocelots and hyenas £10

Tapirs £40

There were also Persian cats ("locomotive rugs") at £3 each – even allowing for the change in the value of money this compares favourably with the £1,000 or more that you would need to acquire a really good specimen of this wonderful animal today. One of these, a white one, was living at Lord Alington's White Farm near Bournemouth in 1892. Elands were £60 each which puts the acclimatisation movement and the eland dinner described in the previous chapter into an interesting perspective. Although these prices were high there was a fierce attrition rate. W. B. Robertson writing in *Chambers's Journal* in 1901, by which time Jamrach was dead and the old St George's East was becoming almost respectable, noted a conversation he had once with him:

> "There's £160 gone," said Jamrach to me once as he handed me a telegram. It ran, "Will accept tapir at 160," and was from Barnum and Bailey. The tapir had died two days previously. Jamrach succeeded in saving £10, however, which he got from an animal stuffer for the carcass.

The same article records that the last thing Jamrach did each day was to complete his "death-book" with the losses running (at cost price not selling value) at between £150 and £200 per month and sometimes significantly more. One 1869 report from the *Daily News* records a visit to Jamrach's shop in which "a tray of dead birds of rare plumage" represents – and here we hear Jamrach's voice – "the losses of a single day." The dead animals were, on occasion, fed to Jamrach's vultures. In his will Charles Jamrach left £6,820 so he died a fairly wealthy man as this is roughly half a million pounds at today's rates.

Birds formed a huge part of the trade and the article pauses to consider the budgerigar. Jamrach probably imported the first live budgerigars into England and paid £26 for a pair selling them on for only £1 profit to a Dr Butler of Woolwich. However, by 1879 they were common and it had also been realised that they would breed successfully in captivity By 1879 Jamrach was buying them by the thousand and exporting them across Europe at eight shillings a pair. At this time in their native Australia they were being sold at sixpence each and bought by the flock to provide a means of livening up shooting parties.

One of the problems for colonists in Australia was that the absence of dangerous big game made it more difficult for them to enact symbolic processes of domination over the animals so they pretended kangaroos were fierce, imported foxes to hunt and, when they were feeling in really dominant mood, they fearlessly blasted budgerigars out of the sky. Vast quantities of birds were leaving Australia at this time. An article in *The Register* for 17th February 1862 mentions ships with 20–30,000 parrots on board leaving Adelaide for London on a regular basis and pointing out that "Thus South Australia is establishing a new export item." This was backed up by canary seed to feed them and this left Adelaide in massive 200- or 400-gallon drums.

Indeed Australia must have been a god-send to Jamrach for it provided not only artifacts such as woomeras and boomerangs for the museum but also a good selection of the livestock downstairs and in the yard. If you wanted to collect an Australian menagerie this is what it would have cost you in 1879:

King parrots £4 per pair
Cassowaries £50 each
Blue cranes £20

Tasmanian crows £2

Kangaroos £25

Wallabies £12

Kangaroo rats £2

Possums £2

Fruit bats £1

Black Swans £5

Wombats £5

The anonymous author of this piece clearly knew a bit about Australian animals. This is what he has to say about a possum he saw:

> [it was] a good deal sleepier than it would have been if at home on that hour of the twenty-four. In that case, instead of snoozing in frost-foggy London daylight, it would have been scampering, growling, up and down a gum-tree by silvery Australian moonlight, swinging from a bough, or seated on it embossed upon a gold onyx sky; or, if a domesticated pet, opening cupboard doors in midnight burglary, and abstracting the contents of the sugar-basin.

Only this morning I was surveying the depredations that the possums have inflicted – as they do every year – on the grape vine which covers the front of my house in northern Sydney and tonight I shall probably be woken – as I am almost every night at this time of year – by possums running about on the roof and even rattling the fly screens on the windows. I am pretty sure from the above description that the author had been in Australia and it is true that there are few things more charming than a possum wandering across your garden with a baby on its back while you are having an *al fresco* evening meal and fewer more cheering sights than a possum silhouetted against a moonlit sky. I can afford to spare them a few grapes.

In addition, Jamrach had many times attempted to acquire koalas but he reported that, so far, none of the specimens he had bespoken from his Australian contacts had managed to survive more than three days at sea. He surmised, probably correctly, that this was because they soon ran out of the fresh eucalyptus leaves that form their sole foodstuff. One imaginative and ambitious trader tried feeding the koalas on eucalyptus throat lozenges and although they did, apparently, eat them they still died at sea.

The Australia trade was also carried out for at least thirty years – from about 1870 – by two English trappers called Walter Payne and Jack Wallace. They were based in Wyndham in Western Australia and by working with indigenous people they caught prodigious numbers of birds especially but also other animals which they sent back to England from the port of Fremantle near Perth. Originally they sold all their stock to other dealers but they then changed their business model and sold direct to the public. They returned to England in 1906 (so slightly after the period covered by this book) with a stock of forty-five kangaroos, twenty wallabies and over 6,000 assorted parrots and lorikeets and set up premises called the Little Zoo on a farm at Lyncombe Hill near Bath. Here they built walled paddocks with shelters for the animals and a state-of-the-art tropically heated nursery for the offspring of their stock. Payne maintained the business in England while Wallace – who, according to a 1907 article in *The Sphere*, said he once went seventeen years without once seeing civilisation – made annual trapping trips to Western Australia. In 1907 they were getting £30 for an adult kangaroo and £5 to £10 for a joey. So, in spite of the fall off in prices of animals from Africa in particular, the British monopoly on Australia had kept the trade in marsupials profitable. Payne and Wallace claimed to be the first people to import antilopine kangaroos into England and these fetched the premium price of £75 a pair. Wallabies and specifically agile wallabies were particularly recommended as good pets. Their Australian depot was at Wild Dog Creek – which is a pretty remote spot – and here they maintained a stock of kangaroos which had been reared in captivity and were therefore tame and good pets. Indeed, visitors to the Little Zoo could feed the kangaroos by hand, with bread being their favourite treat. The business appears to have closed by 1910 or 1911.

The proximity of Australia to Asia made some animals cheaper to buy than they were in Europe and this helped the formation of the collections that were to turn into the four first State zoos. In 1852, for example, an elephant could be had in Sydney for £70 (whereas the Zoological Society of London had recently had to pay £400 for a new elephant for Regent's Park). This was claimed at a meeting regarding the formation of a zoological society in Sydney. If it is true, it shows that there was an elephant in Australia before the one that arrived in Melbourne (bound for the zoo) on the *Cassiope* in

March 1883, which is often assumed to have been the first. In fact, the Sydney elephant arrived on the *Royal Saxon* in 1851 and was kept at the small menagerie run by Messrs Beaumont and Waller on Elizabeth Street together with some monkeys, a pair of lions and some other big cats. These lived in cages on the street during the summer and were moved out to a facility beside the Sir Joseph Banks Hotel in Botany Bay for the rest of the year where they joined a much larger collection including bears and tigers. In the 1850s there was a shop dealing in exotic animals in Sydney's Hunter Street. This was mainly a taxidermist's but included in its stock some exotic birds, a cashmere goat, a Persian goat and a boa constrictor. So although Australia functioned mainly as a source for animals for England it did have a small trade of its own.

Jamrach had many famous customers but perhaps the most celebrated was the Pre-Raphaelite painter, designer and poet Dante Gabriel Rossetti. In 1869 Rossetti acquired his famous wombat, "Top", and this cost him five pounds at Jamrach's. He was a frequent visitor: as his studio assistant Henry Treffrey Dunn recorded, he would drop into the shop "to buy something in the bird or animal line". Rossetti's private menagerie lived in the garden of his large house in Cheyne Walk and the animals I assume he bought from Jamrach included a kangaroo with a joey in the pouch, armadillos, and a raccoon – which frequently escaped and caused havoc with the neighbours' lawns and hen coops. Interestingly enough, apart from the tiger the only other animal known to have escaped from Jamrach was a resourceful raccoon which was never recaptured although there is also a story about an escaped bear which was recaptured when a little girl caught its attention by offering it bread and honey.

Rossetti also had various exotic birds and deer. By no means all of Rossetti's animals were bought from Jamrach and I will deal with other sources – such as beast shows and selling menageries in the pleasure gardens – in later chapters. Rossetti wanted an elephant and Jamrach offered him a small one for £400. But the purchase didn't go ahead either because the price was too steep or because Rossetti had had a rare outbreak of common sense. He also looked into buying a lion was but was put off because he decided he would have to run hot water pipes out into his garden to keep the animal warm in winter. In 1871 he was negotiating to buy a penguin for £10 and was trying to cadge three pounds from his long-suffering but ultra-loyal brother William. The purchase didn't come off and the penguin was sold to Antwerp Zoo which was just as well since, as William himself said, "the penguin, living in so unnatural a condition, will no doubt die almost as soon as it is bought." This was the fate of many of Rossetti's purchases from Jamrach. The famous Top lasted only a couple of months as did a lesser known wombat who succeeded him. More lucky was a woodchuck who seemed to have been more resilient. Turgenev played on the carpet with this woodchuck and it is the subject of a charming sketch almost always erroneously entitled "Rossetti's wombat" by the Pre-Raphaelite follower William Bell Scott.

We saw above that various collectors came to Jamrach to buy exotic animals. Frank Buckland whom we met in the previous chapter was one and became a close friend. Another was Richard Bell whose book *My Curious Pets* listed dozens of animals that had shared his life. He bought a pair of emus for £20. Lord Walter Rothschild also bought from Jamrach to stock his menagerie at Tring and you can still see a stuffed white cougar which is almost certainly the one he acquired from Jamrach in the Rothschild Museum there. Baroness Angela Burdett-Coutts probably bought her llamas from Jamrach's shop. The Prince of Wales, later King Edward VII was a customer and I believe that at least some of the animals collected by Prince Alfred, Duke of Edinburgh, on his famous round-the-world cruise on the H. M. S. *Galatea* found their way to Jamrach's shop. Zoos and museums around the world purchased from Jamrach as well and the Amsterdam Zoological Museum has a stuffed specimen of the now extinct New Zealand Laughing Owl (*Sceloglaux albifacies*). Coincidentally, a specimen of the closely related bird (*Sceloglaux rufifacies*) caused a scandal in 1904 when the New Zealand ornithologist Sir Walter Lawry Buller sold it to Lord Walter Rothschild. It turned out to be cobbled together from half a laughing owl and half of something else. Rothschild wasn't happy and made sure the world knew what Buller, probably unwittingly, had done. More humbly, a monkey which came from Jamrach was sold for £5 from the Ambulance Stall in Stepney Bazaar.

In spite of being based in one of the most notoriously disorderly and crime-ridden areas of London, Jamrach's shop was never the target of burglary or other attempts at theft. This may well have been because he also kept snakes there. In 1879 he had a solitary python wrapped up in a blanket but this might have been enough to put off even the most intrepid intended acts of larceny. The wild animal dealer Joseph Abrahams who operated just down the road from Jamrach at 191–192 St George's Street was actually murdered outside his shop in 1904.

Chapter Two

A story that was widely reported in the newspapers in 1892 (Victorian newspapers tended to reprint the material of other publications without any embarrassment and thus news travelled across the Empire) related to a boa constrictor. Here is the event as recounted by the *Otago Witness* of 17th March 1892:

> One day a celebrated naturalist entered the shop of the late Charles Jamrach, the well-known collector of animals and said: "Now, Jamrach, about the muscular power of the boa-constrictor – I suspect it has been exaggerated."
>
> "Not a bit, sir," said the collector, taking a very fine specimen out of a box.
>
> "He seems very lazy and sleepy," said the professor; "I don't think he could exert himself in this cold climate if he tried."
>
> Jamrach smiled and wound him gently round the professor's body.
>
> "I thought so, Jamrach," he said, "I feel nothing."
>
> But presently he shouted out: "Take him off, Jamrach! Take him off, man; he's strangling me!" So Jamrach just caught hold of the boa's tail and unwound him off the professor ring by ring.
>
> When he had got his breath again the professor admitted there was more "latent muscularity" about the creature than he had suspected.
>
> "Now, sir," said Jamrach afterwards, "that boa was half-asleep and stupid, for he had just swallowed two rabbits, six guinea-pigs [Fluff was lucky!] and 13lb of raw beef …If he had been fasting it's my belief he'd have swallowed the professor himself bodily, for he was a small gentleman."

Fragments like this are all we have of Jamrach's life. We know he smoked cigars. An obituary tells us that he stood six feet tall, "a great big hairy giant, with a jolly laugh, and an unlimited capacity for absorbing liquid refreshment." He referred to his menagerie as "a bit niffy." We know that he had some old Windsor chairs in which he would sit with people like Frank Buckland and the officials and proprietors of the various menageries and zoos discussing prospective purchases, or planning deals by which he would obtain them particular animals. He had a parrot which called "Charlie, shop!" when someone entered the premises (I believe this may later have gone to his neighbour John Hamlyn). He had a good line in yarns and "his morality in most matters was capacious." There is also a delightful vignette of his performance at a party at Frank Buckland's house in 1879 where various collectors and connoisseurs had gathered:

> Genial and good-natured Mr Jamrach, with a diamond brooch on his shirt front and a pleasant smile on his fresh-coloured face, dilated in glowing terms on a Peruvian mummy.

He was married three times. Firstly, to Mary Attanasio (sometimes spelled Athanasio – Mary was from a Neapolitan family although Jamrach's obituary said she was a French Canadian's daughter) then to Ellen Dowling and finally to Clara Salter. These women must have been long-suffering. They had to put up with animals left, right and centre including a sloth which, to one visitor, appeared to live in their private apartments – the Jamrachs actually lived in a cottage in Wellington Road in Bow but presumably, at one time, they had rooms in the shop as well. When Ellen died, Jamrach mused that "she was an excellent woman; unfortunately, however, she did not take very kindly to the animals. Just imagine – she wouldn't even allow the snakes to sleep in her bed in winter time." His first wife had a shock when three lions got out and headed straight for the Jamrachs' parlour in which sat Mary. Jamrach shouted a warning and Mary closed the door which was glass so she had the bracing experiences first of seeing three lions prowling in the hall way and then of realising that the lions could see her. The lions then decided to go upstairs where Jamrach had positioned himself. "Charlie, they are coming upstairs" shouted Mary, upon which Jamrach barricaded himself into a bedroom. So now Jamrach was upstairs and Mary was downstairs and there were three lions loose in the house. The lions then proceeded to wander up and down the stairs with Mary shouting a warning to Jamrach – who kept trying to emerge from his hiding place to deal with them – every time she saw them coming his way. Eventually, the lions all went into the second bedroom and Jamrach deftly locked them in. Here they stayed all day until their regular keeper, a man called Clarke, returned from a day at the docks (the lions appeared to have run off because they were frightened by the sight of Jamrach whom they didn't know) and he coaxed them back into their cages. It is reported that Mary "received a fright on this occasion from which she never properly recovered".

Jamrach died in 1891 by which time the wild animal trade in England was in decline and his stock was much depleted (although his curio and antiquities trade was still going strong). His grave – he was buried with first wife, Mary, as was the standard Victorian custom – is still to be seen in Tower Hamlets cemetery. The main reason for the decline was the opening of the Suez Canal. Until this point, the great majority of ships coming from India and Africa made their first landfall in an English port and so Jamrach had first pick of any animals that might happen to be on board. After that ships might go direct to southern European ports whence their cargoes could be transported overland to, say, Germany. It is worth quoting in full the obituary to Jamrach that was published in Punch on 19th September, 1891 as this shows what a well-known character he was:

> The news on the town like a thunderbolt burst,
> The loss of the Season 'tis reckoned;
> We mourned long ago for King Jamrach the First,
> Now we weep for King Jamrach the Second.
> There's grief at the Zoo, all the lions boohoo,
> And the Elephants dolefully trumpet:
> The Tiger's in tears, and the lonely Koodoo,
> With sorrow's as cold as a crumpet.
> He was seventy-six, but to cross o'er the Styx
> At that age – for a Jamrach – was premature;
> There are lots of young cubs who feel quite in a fix
> At the thought he will not see them mature.
> They howl with wide gorges to think that St George's
> Will see him no more – ah! No, never!
> He will not preside at their shin-of-beef orgies,
> Or nurse them through phthisis or fever.
> The travelling menagerie must wait an age ere he =
> Jamrach – will find any fellow.

The Trade in Exotic Animals

Barnum, 'tis well you are gone we can tell you!

Bison, old boy, do not bellow

There quite so tremendously! Sad, Oh, stupendously!

So is the Ornithorhyncus.

But don't howl the roof off, your anguish is proof of,

Or Regent's Park's swells mad may think us.

Yes, Marsupial Mole, we are "left in the hole,"

But still we must think of our dignity.

Animal sorrow from bardlings must borrow,

The true elegiac benignity.

That Japanese pug I could willingly hug,

He yaps out his grief so discreetly,

And dear Armadillo knows how to sing "Willow,"

Like poor Desdemona, quite sweetly,

My dear Felis Leo, I do feel that we owe

A debt to the urban proprieties.

Don't shame yourself, Ursa, but quite vice versa,

You know how impressive caste's quiet is!

But, Jamrach! O Jamrach! Woe's stretched on no sham rack

Of metre that mourns you sincerely;

E'en that hard nut o' natur, the great Alligator,

Has eyes that look red, and blink queerly,

Mere "crocodile's tears" some may snigger; but jeers

Must disgust at a moment so doleful.

For Jamrach the brave, who has gone to his grave,

All our sorrow's sincere as 'tis soulful.

Jamrach left a dynasty in the form of three sons who maintained the trade – another son George, continued to live on St George's Street but he appears not to have been involved in the family business. James Jacob and Charles, two other sons, also seem to have no involvement in the business. Jamrach had three daughters, Theresa Georgianna (who inherited Jamrach's plate, pictures, furniture and other effects), Albertine and Olymphia.

Chapter Two

Before looking at the Jamrach family dynasty we must note that Charles was not the first Jamrach in England. He arrived on 18ᵗʰ March 1842 (his certificate of arrival – giving his profession as "naturalist" – still survives in the Port of London records) but his elder brother Anton (born 1806) had been working to set up the animal and curiosities trade in East Smithfield since 1839. Unfortunately Anton died in 1841 so Charles was sent to take up where he had left off and this is when the business moved just down the road to St George's Street East. However, Charles did not only take over Anton's business. In 1839 Anton had married Mary Attanasio whom Charles married himself soon after his arrival in London.

Jamrach had three sons in the wild animal trade. The first son was Anton who is the least easy to trace although in 1894 he was listed as having been one of the three great English animal dealers together with his father and Joseph Abrahams. Anton's main trade appears to have been in wild birds and he was quite an authority although he did make the odd error as William Greene ruefully remarked in his *Feathered Friends Old and New* (1896):

> Anton Jamrach rarely made a mistake in picking out a pair for me, but on this occasion he did, for the one he thought was the female moulted into the full male plumage after about six months afterwards in my aviary.

In 1883 Greene's book *Parrots in Captivity* refers to seeing a speaking parrot in Anton's shop "a short time before his lamented death" so the reference above is clearly historical. Anton is also remembered as an important dealer as late as 1904 in a letter to the *Avicultural Magazine*. It is clear that in his earlier days he acted as an agent for his father as an August 1865 issue of the *Adelaide Daily Telegraph* places him in Australia and advertising that he is there to buy Australian animals from his ship the *Coonalto* (on which he had arrived as a steerage passenger in June) or the Port Admiral Hotel. There is also evidence of Jamrach involvement, probably Anton's, in the stocking and establishment of Adelaide Zoo. One poignant memento of the elusive Anton is a clock which was auctioned by Denham's a few years ago where the figures on the face have been replaced by the words ANTON JAMRACH. In fact Anton died in 1885 at the young age of 44 so the reference in Greene is wrong – unless he was referring to the earlier Anton Jamrach – and the clock (which is dated 1885) must be either a mourning piece or something that Anton had had made in the year of his death. Anton's early death created some confusion and Jamrach was forced to place the following notice in the newspapers:

> Mr Charles Jamrach, the noted dealer in wild animals, wishes to say that Anton Herman Jamrach whose death was announced last week, was a son of his, and that he, "the original Jamrach" is still alive, strong and healthy.

We only hear Anton's voice once and that is in the record of a court case heard that the Old Bailey in 1880. It was about stolen sea shells and Anton had been called as an expert witness. He refers to himself as "in partnership with my father as a vendor of wild beasts and dealer in natural curiosities". This suggests that Anton shared the St George's Street East premises with Charles and given the references to him it may be that he specialised in the bird side of the business while Charles dealt with the antiquities and other creatures. In his Old Bailey testimony he certainly suggested this as he went on to add that:

> My father has bought cases with the names of other dealers on them – I have not – it is three years since I had anything to do with shells.

However, although Anton refers to Charles as his father in this testimony they were not, in fact, father and son. Anton's death certificate specifies that his father was actually the Anton Jamrach who died in 1841 so when Charles arrived in England to rescue the business he not only married his elder brother's widow he also took on his nephew – who had been born on 17ᵗʰ November 1841 just under a month after his father's early death – as his step-son. Mary must have been beside herself with grief and anxiety and this act puts the reports of Jamrach's kindness and generosity into sharp perspective.

More substantial in the historical record is Jamrach's son William. He lived at Lordship Road in Stoke Newington and died in 1923. In 1878 he wrote a letter about tapirs to *The Times*. William actually maintained a wild animal business out at Stoke Newington and we know that he was keeping a lion there in 1896 as he sent a card to London zoo stating "Finest lioness in Europe, five years old. £60. Can be seen here." In 1891 he was advertising:

Hungarian Partridges (1000 brace), Waterfowl, Pheasants, Cranes, Wild Turkeys, Wild Animals, Lions, Tigers, Elephants, from a Mouse to a Rhinoceros.

This shows another aspect of the trade which was the provision of large numbers of game birds to stock estates. In 1897 one of William's advertisements offered:

Elephants 3½ ft to 5 ft high, from end of April to July £100 each. Book early.

However, this was after his father's death so he may have started this business quite recently so as not to compete with the family firm. We know that William made several trips to India on behalf of his father who referred to him being in Calcutta in 1869. In 1871 he was again in India and again in 1875. These visits were largely concerned with the purchase of rhinos. In 1872 he bought two rhinos to Berlin Zoo and swapped them for the one that they already had there. In fact, it appears that William visited Calcutta often and may well have had a permanent office there for a *New York Times* report of 21st March 1884 refers to the sale of an elephant to William Cross of Liverpool by "Jamrach of Calcutta". He was also a key figure in the introduction of Muntjac deer to the gentlemanly parks of England. Interestingly although all of Jamrach's living children received something in Jamrach's will, William did not. This may have been because of an estrangement. Equally it may have been that the India business and the growing enterprise at Stoke Newington meant that William had already had his share of the family fortune and so was in no need of further help.

One rather tragic confirmation of William Jamrach's Calcutta business comes to us from reports of the loss with significant deaths among the passengers of the S.S. *City of Agra* (ships named for Agra seem to have been particularly unlucky for the Jamrach family) which foundered off Corunna on 8th February 1897 en route from Liverpool to Calcutta. One of the deceased passengers was Arthur Ernest Jamrach who was noted in *The Times* as the son of William Jamrach of Stoke Newington. We have two fragments which tell of us Arthur's last moments. The first comes from the sole surviving passenger, an Australian called Dunn who was interviewed about the wreck by the *Brisbane Courier* in April 1897. From Dunn we learn that Jamrach was extremely sea-sick on the evening of the wreck and was confined to his cabin. Dunn had sat with him to try to cheer him up but when the ship got into difficulties Jamrach was active in trying to organise the evacuation. From the official inquiry on the loss we learn that Jamrach was seen on deck trying to launch the lifeboats and actually managed to get one into the sea but it could not be got away. When the ship got into difficulties the crew, it appears, jumped into the lifeboats before they were launched and refused to budge leaving the passengers to save themselves. One must assume from the *City of Agra*'s intended route that Arthur was following in his father's footsteps and going to Calcutta on animal-related business.

The final Jamrach to be involved in the animal trade was Albert Edward took over the St George's Street East shop from his father and who died in 1917. He presided over the sad demise of the Jamrach empire which, as has already been noted, had started to decline as the shipping trade changed well within Charles Jamrach's lifetime. This really only affected the wild animal side of the business though and Albert continued to deal in antiquities. But even here the vast scale of the stock became daunting. "Every day," he remarked, some time in 1897, "I vow to buy no more antiquities and every day I break my vow." By 1903 he had abandoned the animal trade altogether citing the prices fetched at an auction in Glasgow where elephants went for only £100 and bears were knocked down at £3 apiece. He added that the regulation of the British steamship lines meant that the captains could no longer carry wild animals for sale as a perk and had to pay freight on them while the foreign firms going into Antwerp and Hamburg did not require this, so prices were cheaper. A puma from South America would cost £40 from the London docks because of the freight charge but he could buy one for £10 in Hamburg.

The prices for animals in 1903 were as follows and it is instructive to compare them with the 1879 price list given above:

Elephants £120 to £150

Lions £20 to £25

Tigers £80

Wolves £4

Hyenas (spotted) £40

Hyenas (striped) £10

Rhinos were still selling at £1,000 and although there had been a rally in the prices of giraffes when the Sudan became impassable because of the war with the Mahdi – they had risen from £50 to £1,000 each – their price was now slipping back to between £300 and £400. The market was also becoming saturated and one of Albert's £10 hyenas had already eaten £60 worth of meat. Several of the later descriptions of Jamrach's establishment, notably those of Sir Garrard Tyrwhitt-Drake, writing in 1946, and Donald Shaw, writing as "One of the Old Brigade" in 1908 are actually accounts of visits when the shop had already passed on to Albert. The obituary for Albert in *The Times* suggests that he kept up the trade in birds even when the animals had gone. However, the obituary in the *Daily Mail* lets Albert speak for himself:

> "The war killed my trade and it is slowly killing me," as he said only a few months ago as we stood beside the empty cages in his formerly wonderful menagerie in St George's in the East. "My heart is broken, my beloved beasts have gone except a few small birds and beasts, and all that is left is the museum of curiosities collected by my father in his travels. Even these I am now selling off, but every time a blue vase or a heathen god leaves its dusty cabinet, I feel as if a part of myself goes with it."

The obituarist sums up:

> He was a cultured, kindly gentleman, generous and simple-minded. He considered his trade not as a tradesman merely, but his heart was in it.

With these sad words ends the Jamrach story although the Jamrachs will occasionally feature again in the treatment of zoos, menageries and natural history museums later in this book. From this history it can clearly be seen just how crucial the contours of Empire and the Imperial trade routes were to the growth and sustainability of the exotic animal supply in England. An Islamist movement takes over the Sudan and the price of giraffes rockets. The English impose tariffs while Continental Europe enjoys free entry of goods and cheaper lions. The agents of a rival power become more numerous in the deserts and jungles and snap up the hippos before the English can get at them.

The Trade in Exotic Animals

To give some idea of the trajectory of the trade one can look at the number of bird and animal dealers listed in the Post Office Directories for London. In 1841 there were just 14, in 1882 there were 81 and in 1895 there were 118 (and this was when the trade was starting to decline). By 1908 there were only 32 left. By 1910 Bostock was stocking his famous Jungle (at that point located in Sheffield) by purchasing animals in Europe and importing them through the inland port of Goole where the inhabitants had the rewarding experience of seeing lions, tigers, bears, wolves, leopards, monkeys and camels being walked through their streets. But twenty years earlier Bostock would have been buying from London.

However, the Jamrachs were not the only people dealing animals on St George's Street East. In fact, there was such fierce rivalry that the various businesses employed the local idlers as runners to and from the docks to inform them of new rarities as they arrived. Charles Jamrach once paid such a runner £5 for his information although the everyday fee was more likely to be one shilling. Dealers also set out in boats to meet the ships as they came up the Thames and even beyond. They spent sleepless nights watching each other's movements and they employed runners to watch each other's runners. This was why it was so important for Jamrach to employ a worldwide network of agents and this, coupled with the travels of his sons Anton and William, was what gave him pre-eminence over his rivals.

Among the main rivals was the murdered Joseph Abrahams who was mentioned earlier. In *Parrots in Captivity*, Greene says that he dealt with Abrahams for years and usually had the comparatively rare Goffin's cockatoo in stock for a few pounds, noting that if he did not have them on any particular day he could always get one "owing to his having correspondents and collectors in every part of the world who are constantly sending him rare birds of every kind." John Bally, who traded from Mount Street, was also in the bird business specialising in the sale of huge quantities of game birds. In April 1856 William Lloyd opened a shop in Portland Road dealing in "Living Marine Animals, Sea-weeds, Artificial Sea-water and marine fresh-water Aquaria". This highly specialised trader catered for the great craze for home aquaria and you could buy exotic crabs for as little as one shilling.

Another dealer was John Hamlyn who traded from 221 St George's Street East where his shop had bird cages hanging outside. Hamlyn was an eccentric character. He had a major business in birds but also kept many

John Hamlyn's shop in 1896 – Hamlyn is looking directly at the camera with his hat in his hand.

other creatures. In 1916 his trade was in decline because of the war but he still found time to eulogise Jamrach and his comments give an interesting insight both into the importance of the Jamrach firm in establishing the animal trade during the Victorian era and also into its sense of itself as a peculiarly British institution:

> The big beast business is, in a word, busted! Elephants, tigers, lions, camels, elephants, rhinos – I never get any of 'em here now. Many's the time I've had giraffes and camels walk into my shop, straight from the dock, lowing their heads as they squeeze through the six-foot door, and then out again at the back, and all settling down and making themselves comfortable. A tight fit, but very homely and satisfying to gaze upon. But I haven't had a camel in my backyard – nothing taller than an emu for years and years! Long before the war the Continent took all that trade and made a corner of what was once an exclusively British business. This was originated by the late Charles Jamrach, the kindest, the sweetest-natured old gentleman who ever looked a man-eating lion in the eye without flinching. When he died, five-and-twenty

years ago, the British trade died with him, and now it's chiefly confined to birds and the smaller animals.

Hamlyn's main claim to fame was the invention of the "Chimps' Tea Party" which was a staple of entertainment in many zoos, notably, London Zoo, when times were simpler. He introduced the Owl-Faced monkey to the country when he sold one to London Zoo and it is still known as Hamlyn's monkey. He and his wife shared the premises with various fully clothed chimpanzees the most famous of which was Gilbert. Gilbert lived in the shop and wore a light blue jersey with the words "H. M. Inexpressible" embroidered in gold in the front and sometimes trousers (but he tended to rip them up). He and Hamlyn would dance together swirling round while Hamlyn cried "Let Joy be unconfined." The other chimpanzees would eat at the table with Hamlyn and his wife and had their own bed in the family's private living accommodation. The business survived the war and Hamlyn even published a *Hamlyn's Menagerie Magazine* but in 1916 his published price list bears out the reality of what he was saying about the decline in the trade with the only animals of real value being an antelope at £25, emus at £12 each, a twelve-foot anaconda at £15 and an eight-foot one at £6. Everything else was of lower value and less interesting and the fact that he was doing a bulk deal on raccoons (selling them at £3 each or £5 for two) shows something of the state into which the business had fallen. Another London dealer who is mentioned at the time was Bruce Chapman.

The ancestor of the London traders was Edward Cross who will be dealt with in more detail in the chapter on menageries as his main activity was as a menagerie proprietor and trading was an offshoot of this business. But in Liverpool his namesake William Cross (they were not related) was a rival to the Jamrachs. Cross's shop was in St Paul's Square and he had a menagerie at Earle Street. He advertised his premises as "The Greatest Zoological Emporium on Earth" and "known throughout the civilised and uncivilised world." In the late nineteenth century he was selling lions, tigers, elephants, camels, bears, wolves and snakes ("by the mile") as he put it. By 1905 his stock list shows how the changes in trade routes which killed off the London trade were also affecting him and he seems to have carried mainly smaller animals and birds – many, like Muscovy ducks or white swans, not very rare. However, his position in Liverpool, which was often a first port of call for ships from the Americas, clearly gave him some advantage as, at a time when the London dealers were finding it hard to get the bigger animals he was still carrying alpacas, pumas, giant turtles, alligators, and Brazilian tortoises (as well as the more common Greek ones), in addition to Amazonian parrots and other jungle creatures such as toucans and tree frogs.

It appears that not all of William Cross's dealings were entirely straightforward. In 1884 he sold an American, Adam Forepaugh's agent, one Samuel Watson, a small elephant engagingly known as "Tiny". By the time "Tiny" reached America he had been transformed into a white elephant charmingly named "The Light of Asia". It transpired that Watson and Forepaugh had painted "Tiny" and that this had caused the poor animal a good deal of pain and blistering. Nevertheless the treatment had continued as there was a good deal of money to be made exhibiting a white elephant and Forepaugh even had four similar elephants in reserve should Tiny die as a result of the poisoning brought on by the paint. We know all this because Forepaugh was prosecuted by the Pennsylvania Society for the prevention of Cruelty to Animals and Cross – who must have been very worried for his good reputation – sent his elephant handlers George Gillespie and Robert Hughes all the way to the Philadelphia in order to testify in the case and help expose the fraud. Devastatingly, Gillespie added that a Mr Fulford, another associate of Forepaugh's, had met him as soon as he had arrived in New York and offered him a large salary to come and work for Forepaugh on condition that he kept quiet about the painting of the elephant. There was always doubt about this elephant and when it first arrived in New York the experts were saying it was an ordinary Indian elephant and at least one sailor had spilled the beans about the painting. Adam Forepaugh was Barnum's great rival and was known to be a shady character. It was said that he had his own gangs of pick-pockets who were paid to work the crowds at his spectacular circus shows.

In 1886 Cross helped the people of Liverpool organise the first ever International Exhibition to be held in that city. His role was to set up an "Indian Village" and to this end he recruited some fifty native Americans to do picturesque things. There was also an animal element and the whole display included zebras and elephants and was housed in what looked like an Indian (i.e. Asian) palace.

An 1887 account of a visit to Cross's shop suggests it was not unlike Jamrach's. The visitor is first struck by the vast number of birds stuffed into cages piled high along the walls. Then there are the lions, jaguars, panthers, bears and, finally, the elephants. Cross had his share of character animals too, such as Chase, the only canine survivor of the ill-fated American Greely Expedition into the Arctic where the explorers ate not only the dogs but also, allegedly, each other to keep going. There was a polar bear possibly going to an Indian prince who collected white animals. There had been a gorilla but it had died of cold and was now stuffed. Cross was also a purveyor of useful animals and claimed that he shipped mongooses a thousand at a time to the sugar plantations of the West Indies where they were plagued by rats and had nothing local as effective as mongooses when it came to keeping on top of them.

Cross's son later helped with the Liverpool business but Cross and Hamlyn were really the last of the great Victorian animal traders and, with their passing, the trade in exotic animals dwindled until the only things left were the tropical birds and fish and the lizards and tortoises which used to be common sights in pet shops although Harrods animal department did occasionally run to leopards and other smaller exotics. Fred Kimber just about comes into our period and maintained a trade until about 1950 in Petersfield, Hampshire, keeping lions in a collection of old railway carriages.

The career of Edward Blyth, a correspondent of Charles Darwin, and curator of the Asiatic Society of Bengal's museum in Calcutta between 1841 and 1863 shows just how much the Imperial network operated to support the exotic animal trade and also something more about its economics. Throughout his career Blyth, who was not a wealthy man, was short of cash and so he supplemented his salary by dealing in wild animals. He offered both Darwin and John Gould specimens of Indian birds which would have been collected alongside his more official activities of obtaining specimens for the museum. Blyth did not have the advantage of proximity to the docks that, say, Jamrach, had and had to bear the advance of costs of shipping and provisioning his finds. He also had trouble with his agents in London and not being on hand could not organise his supply chain. So a mongoose he sent to his agent Bartlett for sale to London Zoo was declined but purchased by Edward Cross for £10. Cross then sold it, more or less immediately, to the zoo for £20. Blyth bought a yak for £25 and offered it to Lord Derby. Derby was only too pleased to send him the £25 but as Blyth had not explained that this did not include the shipping cost he was out of pocket and must have been especially peeved when he saw the greater price for which the yak was knocked down at the great auction of the Knowsley menagerie in 1851. Blyth could, however, sell nearer to home as many of the Indian princes were keen on keeping exotic animals – some of which lived in the women's quarters to entertain their wives – and these were men of extreme wealth who would spend very good money indeed on their hobbies. The Nawab of Oudh, for example, offered £4,000 for a pair of giraffes that could be trained to pull his carriage and Blyth made money from him and profited again when his menagerie was sold off and tigers were to be had for as little as £2 each. The Indian princes were, not unnaturally, especially keen on South American animals which, to them, were as exotic as tigers were to the English and Blyth did attempt to obtain these through his networks for import and sale in India.

Although Blyth was by no means a success in the animal trade he stuck at it and when you consider that he could double his annual salary with one shipment you begin to understand what the economics of this trade really were.

Blyth's story brings together the main themes that structure our under-standing of the animal trade in Victorian England. His position in India uniquely situated him to take advantage of proximity to some of the more desirable animals and he wouldn't have been there had it not been for the Empire. However, he was, for the very same reason, remote from the actual trade and could not generate the economies of scale that Jamrach or William Cross could manage. He had to pay his own shipping costs while the London and Liverpool dealers operated in a world where individual sea captains and sailors took their own risks and so avoided the heavy costs of freight and provisioning. He was also involved in a trade which was not quite respect-able and so could never quite break through in the ways which would have given him more success. The success of Jamrach – who was clearly not a "gentleman" from a Victorian point of view, although he was gentlemanly – was due to his ability to deliver the goods. The connoisseurs, artists and aristocrats who sat in his Windsor chairs did so because they knew that if they wanted, say, a tapir, Jamrach could get it for them and this commercial infallibility appears to have overcome their social scruples. They knew that the wild animal trade was a dirty one and that if they were addicted to the magic of tigers on the lawn then they had to move beyond their usual social circle. They had to expose themselves to unbonneted women and chimpan-zees wearing embroidered jerseys and white-washed elephants.

The Trade in Exotic Animals

The exotic animal trade brings together the potent ingredients of Empire and class and, in that sense, it qualifies as a romance. It was based on hard economics of buying and selling and allowances for deaths and it undoubtedly contributed – as many Victorian fads did: the craze for Scotland, for ferns (*pteridomania*), for orchids, and for collecting the life of seaside rock pools being other examples – to the endangerment of many species. At the same time, the great modern zoological institutions – both the natural history museums and the zoological gardens – could not have established themselves without the existence of the animal traders. As we shall see later – and as we have already seen in the case of Hamlyn's monkey – many of them feature in the stocking of the early zoos in England as well as in continental Europe, the United States of America and Australia. In this sense the trade had some benefits.

So if you were living in Grantham, that hippo you would have seen probably arrived in the squire's park or in the travelling menagerie after having passed though Jamrach's shop. We will now look at the parks and the menageries themselves.

CHAPTER THREE

The Travelling Menageries - The Only Dead Elephant in the Fair!

On 2ⁿᵈ May 1833, when William IV still reigned and his niece Victoria was still just a pretty princess waiting for her Prince, two angry and frightened elephants were rampaging down the Oxford road from Reading to Henley. They had smashed their travelling wagon and had overturned several others. In their wake was a rolling brawl. Fists were flying. Whips were cracking hard on flesh. Crowbars and tent poles were making sickening or encouraging impacts (depending on whether you were victim or aggressor) on skulls. A man of over thirty stones in weight had armed himself with a hook and was fighting with a man of only five stones in weight who was trying to whack him with one of the mallets used to drive in the gigantic tent pegs that kept the big marquees stable. One caravan was on fire and two children in night gowns were being carried to safety by some local villagers who had come either to see the fun or to join in. Lions and tigers were roaring, a rhinoceros was stamping up and down in his cage and a giraffe was peering timidly down at the mayhem below.

What was happening here was, very simply, a trade dispute. Wombwell's menagerie had left the Mayday Fair at Reading early in order to get a good pitch at the Henley Fair which started on the 3ʳᵈ and where it was first come first served for the most lucrative and favoured spots. Wombwell's was the largest menagerie on the circuit and this branch of it (there were three in all by 1833) was the most significant. In hot pursuit was Hilton's (also referred

A TICKET FOR WOMBWELL'S MENAGERIE

to as Hylton's) menagerie which was nowhere near as big, although it had the biggest elephant, and so was more reliant on a good pitch to attract custom than was Wombwell's. Travelling lighter, the Hilton's caravans gradually gained on Wombwell's procession and the lead wagons started to try to overtake their rivals. The Wombwell's men took spoiling action and used their wagon to block the road. In a slow motion anticipation of the chariot race in *Ben Hur*, the drivers started lashing at each other and eventually one of Wombwell's men was knocked from his seat by a well-aimed tent-pole. That did it and the employees of each menagerie, including the denizens of the respective freak shows, swarmed from their caravans and laid into each other. In the midst of all this Wombwell's elephant wagon overturned and its inhabitants smashed their way out and made of down the road breaking everything in their way. The children saved from the burning caravan were "Lord" George Sanger and his brother William who went on to be important menagerie keepers in their own right.

Travelling menageries were a popular and familiar feature of the Victorian scene and traversed the country year in year out setting up at fairs or simply being an entertainment in themselves. The main ones were Wombwell's and, later, Bostock's but Manders's, Day's, Symons's (probably a small offshoot of Mander's), Batty's and Hilton's were also important, while Crockett's was a small exhibition of snakes, crocodiles and human freaks. In its prime Wombwell's (which was subsequently sold to Bostock) had over 500 animals in its main show and its popularity meant that, at its height, it was organised as three separate and each significantly large shows known as No1, No2, and No3 respectively. Few parts of the country were not within a walk of a menagerie on at least one day a year and the fairs which marked the rhythms of rural life and acted as the labour exchanges for the agricultural economy would often include a menagerie. When Gabriel Oak. the protagonist of Hardy's *Far from the Madding Crowd*, stands in his smock hoping to be hired as a shepherd at the Casterbridge Fair we should imagine that his soundscape included not only the bleating of sheep and the lowing of cattle but also the roaring of lions and the trumpeting of elephants. The urban fairs in, for example, London, Glasgow, and Nottingham were also the regular stopping places of the menageries which, between them, offered almost everyone some opportunity to see exotic animals. You didn't even have to have any money as you could see the animals as they travelled in their purpose-built and often massive wagons or, if you couldn't afford to go into the tents to see the special exhibitions of lion taming and other circus-like performances you could simple walk around the cages and peer in at their inhabitants.

Wombwell charged one shilling (5p) to go into his main enclosure with a reduced rate of 6d (2.5p) for anyone deemed to be a labourer, tradesman or servant. Children also got in for 6d. This lower charge for working people does not appear to have applied all day but to have been timed to enable them to come to see the menagerie after work and, as we shall see, this was a strategy eventually adopted by various zoological gardens and natural history collections. However, the standard price of one shilling shows that the menagerie expected a reasonable degree of patronage from the middle and upper classes and the evidence suggests that this was indeed the case. It is also not surprising, as there is no reason to think that the gentry were not every bit as curious to see and enjoy rare animals as their humbler neigh-bours and if you didn't have easy access to a zoo or private collection then the menagerie was the only place you could do this. Wombwell's prices may be put into perspective when they are compared with the cost of hiring the cheapest seat with a reasonably unobstructed view of Queen Victoria's funeral cortege in 1901. This was six pounds in a temporary grandstand erected in Buckingham Palace Road. The seats in the stands outside the clubs were selling – and with high demand – at £150 each. This was just to see the procession go by and conferred no rights to attend any of the services or other ceremonies. A common and liveable wage at the time was one pound per week and that had to cover the four staple features of the Victorian poor's budget: rent, food, the boot club and burial insurance.

However, although the zoos were frequently in difficult financial straits and many had to close soon after their foundation for lack of money, the menageries appear to have represented a far sounder business proposition. In the 1870s, for example, Bostock was making over £1,000 from each exhibition (at least £100,000 at today's values as much of the money was held in gold sovereigns). Wombwell left not only these three menageries but also significant cash bequests of £100 each as well as two annuities of £10 each and substantial stock holdings. Big money could be made at the fairs. For example, at the 1828 Bartholomew Fair the takings of the four menageries that were exhibiting were as follows: Wombwell's £1,700, Atkins's £1,000, Morgan's £150 and the much smaller Ballard's £90 (but even that represents about £9,200 at today's values so was a pretty good return especially as Ballard's smaller stock meant lower overheads).

The reason for the superior financial performance of the menageries over the zoos is probably due to their superior power in attracting paying customers. Although the menageries had high overheads and high risks in maintaining a fleet of specialist vehicles and the draught animals and, later, steam engines and lorries to pull them, they brought the animals to the customers and did not have to depend on repeat business more than once a year. In addition, the fact that they were almost always attached to larger fairs and circuses meant that they had a ready-made set of added attractions for which, unlike the zoos, they didn't have to pay themselves. Finally, the peripatetic nature of menageries made them moving targets for taxation and licence fees. One of Bostock's complaints when he finally hung up his whip in 1931 was that taxes were driving him out of business. However, a business that lasted, as did the Wombwell–Bostock combination from 1805 to 1931, was clearly a good money-maker and the evidence is that the other major menageries enjoyed similar profitability. For example, Manders's managed to carry on in pretty good shape until 1937 when it was sold out to Fred Kimber (the Petersfield-based animal dealer whom we met in the previous chapter. Together with his son, Fred kept an animal show going – including a regular spot on Paignton Pier – until 1955.

The Travelling Menageries – The Only Dead Elephant in the Fair

If menageries were not part of bequests or sold trunk, horn and claw they were auctioned off and we have good records of at least two major sales. It is instructive to compare the prices realised on those occasions with the prices at the Knowsley sale (given below) or those charged by Jamrach or Cross in their shops. In 1872 Wombwell's No 1 menagerie was sold at auction in Edinburgh. The first lot was a raccoon which went for the modest price of £1 but to a very good home as the buyer was none other than the great Archibald Primrose, 5th Earl of Rosebery and a man who was fortunate enough to achieve all three of his stated ambitions in life (to win the Derby, to marry an heiress and to be Prime Minister). A Tasmanian Devil went to a Mrs Day (I assume of Day's menagerie) for £3 and 5 shillings (£3.25). Jamrach bought a small drill monkey for five guineas (£5.25) but Charles Rice spent £68 and eighteen shillings (£68.90) on a pair of mandrills, two Anubis baboons and five dog-faced baboons. An emu, described as "a very suitable bird for a gentleman's park and a nice show thing for the ladies after breakfast" went for £7 while Jamrach spent £13 on a pair of pelicans who had been trained to run races and were described as originally from Knowsley although as that collection had been broken up some twenty-one years earlier this seems unlikely. The bigger animals fetched substantial sums. Jamrach bought a llama for £15, three leopards for £60, a lion for £200, a tiger for £155 and a bear for five guineas (£5.25). Not to be outdone, Rice bought the biggest lion for £185, two more for £140 each, another two smaller ones for £90 each, a lioness for £80 and a kangaroo for £12. A rare black-maned (probably a Barbary) lion went to Bristol Zoo for £270 and a black-maned lioness was sold to Belle Vue Zoo for 100 guineas (£105). Finally, Rice spent £85 on a gnu, £50 on a zebra and £145 on a small elephant. The biggest price of all was the £680 paid for the male elephant that was destined for Belle Vue Zoo. Rice alone spent nearly £1,086 in one day and that did not include commissions or the cost of getting his animals back to London (and then, probably, on to his brother-in-law in Hamburg) and this reinforces the scale of the trade at this point. The prices also put into perspective the £500 that a lion cost at the beginning of the century and show that although lions were still expensive commodities they were becoming more common and this was driving prices down.

In 1875 Frank Buckland attended the sale of Manders's menagerie in Islington (this was the original menagerie, another menagerie toured for many years subsequently under the names of Manders's Royal Star Menagerie, Manders's Grand Star Menagerie and Manders's American Jungle). He recorded the following prices:

Two lion cubs £150

A pregnant lioness £150 (her keeper opined *sotto voce* that whoever bought her wouldn't get the cubs as "she'll eat the lot, she's the wust mother out")

Another lioness £30

A hyena £5

A panther £12

A jaguar £30

Another jaguar £32

A mating pair of Tasmanian Devils £6

A wombat £5 ten shillings (£5.50)

A racoon, five monkeys and a cat £3

Another racoon 8 shillings (40p)

A mongoose £1 2 shillings (£1.10)

A mandrill £105 (with a "diabolical low forehead, like the demons in Fuseli's pictures")

A Canadian bear £1 6 shillings (£1.30)

A Russian bear £1. This bear was called Johnny and was a great favourite. His keeper Bob almost wept when he was knocked down for only a pound. Bob asked Frank if he would buy him and make a present of him but although Frank did consider it (not to give to Bob but to kill and stuff) he didn't as the bear's teeth were gone and he had a moth-eaten coat. Bob used to dance with Johnny and he told Frank that "he has nursed me in his lap more often than my mother."

A zebra £30

A Java hare £2

An opossum 11 shillings (55p) – and this was a rare black one too

A jackal 5 shillings (25p)

Three cockatoos £1 ten shillings (£1.50)

A talking cockatoo £1

A macaw 4 guineas (£4.20)

A pelican £4 5 shillings (£4.25)

A camel £7 10 shillings (£7.50). This was a very bad-tempered animal and later that year created mayhem at a show in Framlingham when he bit his keeper and caused such a commotion that people thought the lions were out and general panic ensued.

Another camel £1 (clearly a poor specimen)

Another camel £20

Another camel £20

A camel calf £21

A llama £16 10 shillings (£16.50)

Two goats £3

A sheep £1 5 shillings (£1.25)

The main bidders at this sale were Jamrach and Rice with Bostock bidding on behalf of Wombwell's menagerie (which later advertised that its collection had been vastly enriched "by extensive purchases at the late sale of Manders' menagerie"). Nevertheless the prices were low and the whole collection realised only £1,200 which included £40 for a painted carriage which Bostock recycled for his own show and £95 for Manders's living caravan

THE ROYAL FAMILY AT THE MENAGERIE IN 1847

which also went to Bostock. The sale was prompted by desperation as the menagerie was going broke and the auction was without reserve. Nevertheless there are great discrepancies between the prices realised here and those at the Wombwell show only three years earlier. Buckland's anecdote about Johnny the bear and the fact that the show had hit hard times suggest that many of the animals were not at their best.

The success of the menageries depended on large numbers of customers paying a modest entry fee. However, the Royal family were very keen on Wombwell's and there were command exhibitions in 1830 (for Princess Victoria), in 1834 (for King William IV and Queen Adelaide) in 1847 and 1854 (for Queen Victoria and Prince Albert) and in 1869 for the now widowed Queen and her children. These performances are what gave Wombwell's (by now Edmonds's) the right to call itself "The Royal Menagerie". The shows in 1847 and 1854 took place in the quadrangle of Windsor Castle and the

STAFFORDSHIRE FIGURE OF POLITO'S MENAGERIE

1854 occasion is especially well documented. Queen Victoria walked round the menagerie twice accompanied by the proprietor Edmonds and the entire Royal family came along too together with assorted grandees both British and European. Ieemonah, the biggest elephant, was fed from a bag of buns by the young Prince of Wales and then ridden round the quadrangle by Wombwell's star lion tamer Ellen Chapman. The Queen, perhaps fearing disaster, did not, however, want to see Ellen's performance with the big cats. After the Royal family had withdrawn, the castle's servants and retainers were allowed to look round the menagerie as were nearly 700 boys who were invited up from Eton College together with their Head Master. They got to see the lion-taming act which was accompanied by patriotic music from the menagerie band (bands were a very important part of the menageries and often mentioned as a chief attraction – the fabulous and very rare Stafford-shire flatback ornaments of both Polito's and Wombwell's menageries show the bands very prominently and one wonders if these wonderful objects were made for sale at the menagerie shows).

The menagerie managers then had dinner in the steward's room while the staff chowed down in the servants' hall.

The Queen then requested that the animals stay overnight so that she could see them by lamplight. She also asked – perhaps buoyed up by the whisky-laced claret that was one of her favourite tipples – to see the lion-taming act which she watched from the castle windows. It is difficult not to be touched by these scenes and the enjoyments of different times. The shows coincided with the Windsor Michaelmas fair and in 1847 it appears that a personal visit by Colonel Phipps, Prince Albert's private secretary, was what led to the request that the show visit the quadrangle before leaving town. An image of the 1847 visit shows the Queen and her family looking at a caparisoned elephant ridden by a woman wearing an elaborate ostrich feather headdress. The surviving image of the 1854 visit is even more charming and shows Edmonds in the private chambers of the castle with the Royal children playing with a collection of especially winsome lion and tiger cubs among whom are almost certainly the "ligers" which had been born at Appledore in Kent earlier that year. The Royal family had a weakness for ligers and when some were born in Atkins's menagerie while it was lodged at Windsor in 1828 the cubs were presented to a delighted George IV who was always pleased to see something unusual.

The touring menageries started their long journey during the eighteenth century. George Wombwell, who was born in 1777, started touring in 1805 having previously built up a collection which he showed first at Smithfield and Bartholomew Fair in 1804. His business was based in Commercial Road, which is not far from the docks and therefore was a direct precursor of Jamrach's. Wombwell certainly used this proximity to buy animals direct from ships coming into the Port of London. In fact, his business seems to have started when he bought two boa constrictors off the docks for seventy guineas (£73.50) and started showing them for money in pubs. He appears to have kept doing this even after the menagerie proper was on the road as in 1807 we find someone (almost certainly George Wombwell) in Bristol showing two boa constrictors in the White Swan and advertising as a buyer for any "foreign birds or curious animals." Like Jamrach and the other East End dealers, Wombwell eventually had a network of agents keeping an eye out for likely animals arriving in both London and Liverpool and buying them on his behalf for the menagerie.

But Wombwell was not the first of the touring menagerists. By 1799, George Pidcock was already in the business and we have an account of his touring show's visit to Ipswich in 1800. Another menagerist, Perry, appears to have been on the road as early as 1744 and was exhibiting the biggest menagerie at Bartholomew Fair in 1748. Perry was based at the White Swan in Holborn and in the same year there were menageries on display at the White Horse in Fleet Street and the Flying Horse on Bishopsgate Street. These menageries were mainly composed of big cats although Perry's also had a camel. At this time, pubs were clearly an important site of encounter with exotic animals. As we shall see later, one of the most durable of the Victorian private zoos, Belle Vue in Manchester, started with a display in the proprietor's pub and before zoos arrived in Australia the best place to see exotic animals was the Sir Joseph Banks Hotel in Botany Bay where Messrs Beaumont and Waller kept their menagerie. Pidcock, and later Polito, were the proprietors of the Exeter 'Change, the largest fixed private zoo in London and were obviously trying to get the best value from their stock by taking it on the road. Another menagerist of this time was called Miles and his name is sometimes found in association with Pidcock's and at other times, for example in the list of menageries at Bartholomew Fair in 1799, independently. These early menagerists establish a model for Wombwell and, subsequently, Thomas Atkins to follow. Although Atkins reversed Pidcock's and Polito's practice by converting his travelling show into a fixed zoo.

Another early menagerie was Ballard's and this appears to have been much smaller that Wombwell's or Atkins's. It first shows up at Bartholomew Fair in 1810 but its main claim to fame was a notorious incident in 1816 when one of its lions escaped and became a highwayman. It lay in wait by the roadside and attacked the Exeter Mail Coach just outside Salisbury. The lion killed a horse and a dog but the entreaties of Ballard himself stopped the coach's guard – one Joseph Pike, who went on to make a small reputation from the incident – from shooting it with his blunderbuss. The lion, cried Ballard, had cost him £500. Once the lion was secured another horse was found and the coach trotted on. In 1825 Ballard was still exhibiting this lion and trading off its infamous past.

The rivalry between menageries didn't always result in the kind of fracas on the Oxford Road described above. In about 1830 (this is one of those stories which feel too good to be true) Wombwell had just finished setting up his show when his elephant dropped dead. The other menagerist at the fair was Thomas Atkins who gleefully put up a sign advertising his pachyderm as "The Only Live Elephant at the Fair." But Wombwell was not dismayed and, having erected a tent around the carcass of his creature, put up a rival sign advertising "The Only Dead Elephant at the Fair." You could see live elephants any day reasoned Wombwell but dead elephants were not something you came across on every corner. Wombwell and Atkins struck up a gentleman's agreement to exhibit at the large fair at Croydon on alternate years.

Wombwell's menagerie eventually grew so large that it was split into three. No. 1 was taken over by Wombwell's wife following his death in 1850 and was then continued by her second husband Alexander Fairgrieve. It was eventually sold at the auction in Edinburgh in 1872 although a subsequent No. 1 menagerie toured under the management of "Captain" Fred Wombwell and, in 1897, was set up in Glasgow as a permanent exhibition known as The Scottish Zoo. No. 2 was maintained by Wombwell's niece Mrs Harriet Edmonds until 1884. It then carried on under the Bostock name until it was auctioned off in 1896. However, another No. 2 menagerie started more or less immediately as the old No. 3 – which was managed by Wombwell's nephew George to whom it had been bequeathed – was renumbered. This menagerie was on permanent display in London in 1897 and 1898 after which it toured Europe until 1906 when it was auctioned off in Paris. Although we have some documentation relating to Wombwell as well as a vast quantity of newspaper reports, the underlying position for research into his menagerie is still developing and separating fact from the many good stories told by early commentators such as Thomas Frost in his books *Old Showmen and the Old London Fairs* (1874) and *Circus Life and Celebrities* (1881), which are good sources for the traditions but not necessarily to be taken at face value, is an ongoing task. As the successor to Wombwell, Bostock takes the story to its end and the menagerie finally closed in 1931 with most of the stock being sold at giveaway prices to London Zoo.

Day's menagerie appears to have been formed from Wombwell's original No. 3 show and then probably supplemented by purchases from the sale of No. 1 although it is not mentioned as an independent entity until 1866. It was attracting little interest when it exhibited at Bartholomew fair in 1873 but was clearly still a draw in the countryside. By 1889, Day's had 500 animals and an article in the *Oxford Chronicle* describing the St Giles Fair that year says that the menagerie "was filled from morning to night". A photograph of Oxford's St Giles Fair in 1895 shows Day's menagerie with the typically gaudy facade of the main tent painted with scenes that one suspects were considerably more thrilling than the reality (except when one of the lion tamers had an accident), a barker and drummer, a pierrot, an

DAY'S MENAGERIE AT ST GILES'S FAIR IN 1895

awning concealing what I suspect is the band and a lone pelican gazing down at the crowd.

The thought of what was going through that pelican's mind and what I could know of its life when I first saw that photograph some six or seven years ago was one of the stimulants to this research.

Batty's menagerie was London based and appears to have been attached to Astley's amphitheatre (see the later chapter on circuses). A scrap from a street ballad recorded by Henry Mayhew in *London Labour and the London Poor* (1861–1862) shows that it took part in at least one Lord Mayor's Show procession:

> A day like this we never saw,
> The truth I am confessing,
> Batty's astonishing menagerie
> Is in the great procession;
> There's lions, tigers, bears and wolves,
> To please each smiling feature,
> And elephants in harness drawing
> Drury Lane Theatre!

Batty's also toured extensively and on one of its visits to Tregaron in mid Wales in July 1848 an elephant died, allegedly after drinking water from a stream contaminated with lead from the nearby mines. It is said he was buried behind the Talbot Hotel which still stands and in which, during the long hot summer of 1976, I used to sit drinking with the itinerant Australian and New Zealand sheep shearers who, in those days, followed summer (and the wool season) round the world and waited in the bar for the local farmers to hire them at rates that the Welsh labourers could only dream of. A recent archaeological dig attempted to locate the elephant's skeleton but although nothing was revealed it may be that the extreme acidity of the local soil had removed the remains. The idea that menageries seeded the island with dead elephants is not unique to Tregaron. There is a mound in a field beside the A15 in Lincolnshire just opposite the Tally Ho! Inn on the outskirts of Sleaford. This is reputed to be the grave of a menagerie elephant that was buried there some time in the nineteenth century. But, unlike the Tregaron story, which has some corroboration, this remains a charming and poignant legend and I have found no reference to a menagerie losing an elephant while touring Lincolnshire.

Dead elephants, whether buried or on display, are, of course, much less hazardous than live animals escaping from their cages. All the menageries seem frequently to have suffered from this problem and the difficulties of securing large numbers of animals (at the height of his career Bostock probably had about 2,000 on the road) in travelling cages were not inconsiderable. In May 1857 William Manders looked out of his caravan window and saw not only the picturesque landscapes of the Derbyshire Peak District but also his nightwatchman struggling weakly with an escaped gorilla while two other gorillas watched contentedly from the canvas roof of the main menagerie tent. Manders chased the gorilla off with a hammer and it shinned up a pole to join its friends. The three then set off across the roof of the elephant wagon (no doubt waking its snoozing inhabitants and adding to the commotion) and loped off down the road to Belper. Here they were recaptured but not before a Hammer Horror mob of scythe- and pitchfork-wielding villagers had joined in the fray.

A little known menagerie was George Whittington's. This was based in Sheffield and toured between 1861 and 1871 when it sunk under the weight of a court case brought by Whittington against the members of a mob who had sought revenge for a child whose arm had been amputated after a savaging by Whittington's leopard. The mob attacked and smashed up the show when it was based in Tipperary and Whittington got scant redress from a hostile Irish court. But his menagerie had some form. A lion escaped and killed two dogs in 1868 and the very next year the lion carriage overturned and the lions got out again. In 1869 a wolf escaped in Liverpool and attacked the menagerie's monkeys and then the nightwatchman (being a menagerie nightwatchman was plainly a risky job). It was driven off with a pitchfork and lassoed by Whittington himself. In fact, 1869 was a stupendous year, for the lion tamer, Joseph Pearce, was also badly mauled by a puma and only saved when a lioness joined in and set about the puma. All this was in front of the paying customers. In 1864 these customers were especially disgusted (one suspects somewhat pruriently) when Whittington was at Glasgow and Dundee. Here he offered show where two "Zulus" bit the heads off live rats, skinned them with their teeth and ate them raw. Tom Norman, the "Silver King", later had a show involving a Mrs Barker who used to bite the heads off of live rats and also a group of retired sailors who were painted black and exhibited as savage Zulus so one wonders if this is where he got the idea. Norman became a specialist circus and menagerie auctioneer and is best remembered today because the famous Elephant Man passed through his extensive network of freak shows. The bad publicity Whittington's show attracted caused it to be suppressed but the report of its visit to Dundee is interesting as another menagerie is mentioned – a much more refined one – Steven's, which is otherwise entirely obscure. Whittington's was obviously and small and ill-equipped show with not many animals (my guess is that it only had some big cats, wolves, bears and monkeys) but its fleeting appearances (and that of Steven's) suggests there are more menageries yet to be discovered.

There were also special occasions like the Great Exhibition or the great fair in Hyde Park which was held in 1838 as part of the celebrations surrounding the coronation of Queen Victoria. Here both Wombwell's and Hilton's menageries were on display together with what was one of the very last performances of Mrs Stevens, the celebrated "pig-faced lady", which gives a flavour of the last of the old Regency-style exotic animal shows. Mrs Stevens was actually a bear who had had its faced shaved and was dressed as a lady and kept strapped to chair under which lurked a boy with a stick. The showman would ask Mrs Stevens questions and the bear would grunt along depending on how many times and how ferociously the boy poked it. These shows were stopped, for humanitarian reasons not long after and throughout the century one finds a gradual advance of humanitarian sentiments both in the courts where the RSPCA (founded in 1824 as the SPCA) prosecuted cases of direct cruelty in menageries and circuses and in the public discourse where an increasingly liberal establishment voiced doubts not only about performing animals but also about the general principle of keeping wild and noble animals in cages. Wombwell himself came in for severe criticism over the lion fight described in a subsequent chapter. This took place in 1825 and it is almost inconceivable that such an event could have happened twenty years later. This kind of entertainment was offset by a more explicitly educational aim represented by the pamphlets and descriptive catalogues that some of the menageries published for sale to their customers. These were very similar to the early zoo guide books described later and often included, as did the guides, some account of how the different animals had been acquired by the menagerie.

In 1843 Wombwell was the subject of a verse by Charles Clark "the bard of Totham" who was a tenant farmer with a taste for poetry and who combined self-publishing on his own private press with an eclectic range of other publishing and collecting interests. The poem is riddled with dreadful puns but it shows how celebrated Wombwell was in his day:

Hail! Hail! to thee Wombwell! Of Menagerists the prince,
Whene'er again you visit us all must their joy evince;
And such the fame of him whose Show all love to set their eye on,
If once "an Essex calf" Great Sir, you've long become a "lion!"

Yes, in Essex, and at Braintree, – in a cot no longer seen –
Famed Wombwell, there the wight (we've read) was born at
　　Beckwith Green;
And if e'er the goddess of the morn hail 'tis not surprising,
For, they say, unto A roarer you owe all your early rising!

If rum-maging their pedigree, we see, when we begin,
What numbers of the famed have sprung from humble ori-gin,
And while many are the methods which, to rise in life, men take,
Yours' was – to never ne asleep when others "kept a wake!"

We come up when you "come down" and you smile to see us
　　then, -
'Tis here (Bunyan-like) we've "lighted on a place where is a den."
Within you've such variety, that – if honest – 'tis no sin
To think, "from Indus to the Pole," you "take each creature in!"

And the animals at Wombwell's, oh! How tractable they are,
Whenever – lawyer-student-like – they're "called to the bar;"

But we hate the "cut" that "comes again" when from a keeper's
　　stick, -
So let not e'en the slow so oft be "cut unto the quick!"

I'd not, howe'er, have visitors make free when in their mirth,
Lest they should quickly wish to be deliver'd from their berth,

And that such rash acts to lament we never may be cause,

May – when we wish to handle them – the thought e'er give us
pause!

When your Menagerie we're in, that you'd serve us, who can
doubt;

Though by bands – as if offended – it appears, you'd "serve us
out:"

While so many are the trumpets, Sir, that for you still are blown,

You can have no occasion, sure, to ever "blow your own!"

O! Your visits, Sir, amongst us, much more frequent may they be;

And "well-favour'd" too – as Joseph – may you we ever see!

Long with Wombwell's fame – at Fair time – still may our ears
be dinn'd,

While he's the current gaining by which men "raise the wind!"

The travelling menageries were often unpopular because of the enormous
disorder that they were often seen as bringing to the towns they visited and
we have already seen the case of the great battle on the Oxford road. More
commonly, disorder took the form of accidents and disasters (we will see
later how peculiarly prone to fires the circuses which were often attached to
the menageries were) as well as crimes. To see how prevalent this disorder
was I looked at every reference to menageries in forty-nine British regional
newspapers and *The Times* for the years 1850–1855. During this time there
were competing journalistic attractions such as the Great Exhibition and the
Crimean War. Over the five year period there were seventy-six reported
accidents or offences at menageries and this, taking into account the
Victorian habit of repeating the same story from newspaper to newspaper
translated into some 600 reports of crimes at menageries. This is from a total
of roughly 1600 reports on menageries – so over a third of all reporting
concerned crimes or accidents.

The incidents split into three main categories: people (these could be either
spectators or menagerie employees) being attacked by animals, animals
escaping and causing mayhem, and theft using the menagerie as a cover.
There were also three cases of menagerie proprietors being prosecuted for

obstructing the highway. The same kinds of crimes and accidents in menageries abroad were also reported – the most bizarre one being the theft of a lion from the Parisian *Jardin des Plantes*. The only clues were a trail of blood and bloody handkerchief embroidered with the initials *VC* – one Aberdeen newspaper wryly observed that it was more likely that the lion had stolen the thief.

In addition, menageries could be on the periphery of other crimes. For example on 2nd February 1850 some employees of Wombwell's menagerie were enjoying a quiet pint in a Liverpool pub when some American sailors came in and, being used to a segregated society one assumes, took exception to the fact that one of Wombwell's men was black. A fight ensued and the result was that the Americans got a swingeing fine from the magistrates who opined that behaviour of this kind was not acceptable in England. Indeed one feature of menageries was that they brought a greater racial diversity to the English countryside than was usually the case. Menageries were sites where the races mixed. In rural England you might well only see a non-white face when the menagerie arrived. The enlightened attitude taken by the Liverpool magistrate, who was in a port where racial diversity had long been a feature of life, is one thing but when an Indian animal handler was severely injured in the provinces only one man would take him into his house where many refused and this was praised as an act of Christian charity. Pablo Fanque the circus entrepreneur was born in Norwich but his father was an African house servant. Animal trainers in the menageries and circuses who were of African heritage included Martini Maccomo, an Angolan, who worked the lions and tigers in Manders' and then Bostock's menagerie and survived at least one nasty moment when his animals got out of control.

Maccomo was a Victorian personality and the most famous of the many well-known lion tamers. His successor Sargano (William Dellah) was less lucky and was mauled to death by two bears and a hyena. Charles Wood was attacked by a bear at Day's menagerie while Alexander Young, Alexander Beaumont and Marcus Orenzo were attacked by their lions. Martin Largue, Richard Jorgnis (performing as Dacoma), Joseph Ledger, John Humphries (performing as Alicamousa), and Martin Bartlett worked with big cats while Hezekiah Moscow worked with bears and Ledger Delmonico with hyenas. Ephraim Thompson specialised in elephants. So from the point of view of an English villager or the citizen of a provincial town the menagerie was not only an opportunity to see exotic animals but also a place to meet (and

MACCOMO

be frightened by) Africans. The association of menageries with Africans can also be seen from the cover of the sheet music of the popular song *Manders's Menagerie or Come and See the Guinea Pigs* which was published in 1876. This shows two cartoon African barkers. One is an adult dressed as a typical "black and white minstrel", the other is a child dressed as a pierrot and banging a drum. The chorus of the song is a far-fetched account of the pleasures of a menagerie:

> Come and see the winkles, come and see the whales,
>
> Come and see the guinea pigs in mourning for their tails,
>
> Come and see the kangaroo that's learning how to shoot,
>
> Come and see the crocodile that plays upon the flute.

They are placed in front of a backdrop which has pictures of most of these remarkable creatures and which parodies the kinds of elaborate cloths or painted boards that the menageries did use to drum up trade. The lyric also stresses the animal performances available at the menageries and this remained an important aspect of their charms and a distinguishing feature from most zoos throughout their existence.

Menageries clearly constituted sources of crime and one can see scattered references to a popular revulsion in the newspapers. The police in some towns clearly saw them as sources of nuisance and dens of illicit gambling. Sanger gives an account of a huge riot when the menagerie was at Lansdown Fair in Bath. A drunken mob led by the fearsome red-head "Carrotty Kate" wrecked the Fair but were then chased down by bare-back riders from the menagerie (which they had spared) and were then flogged and half-drowned in a muddy pond by the irate stall holders. No wonder people wrote to local newspapers saying how much they dreaded the annual visit of the menagerie with its attendant dangers and crimes – indeed one letter pointed out that one attraction stressed by the menagerie barkers was the danger posed by escaping animals. One case of damages for an accident included the fact that the plaintiff could not have been as hurt as he was claiming as he had been seen strolling round Wombwell's menagerie and thus committing a fraud. A magistrate's court dealing with a pick pocket apprehended at a menagerie elicited the alarming confession that he was part of a gang which followed the menagerie round the country which seems to bear out the popular opinion of the troubles menageries caused.

One writer pointed out that the child lion tamer used by Wombwell was in nightly danger of death and asked if it would be wrong for Wombwell to be hanged for murder if this happened – as indeed it did to the celebrated lion tamer, Ellen Bright, the "Lion Queen", who, on 14th January 1850 while Wombwell's was based at Chatham, provided her charges with a free supper at the tender age of 17. Interestingly enough after Bright's fatal mauling by her tigers – which was memorialised in a stirring Staffordshire figurine – Wombwell prominently advertised that he had bought more tigers. A law was passed making it illegal for women to be lion tamers but this seems to have had little effect as a second "British Lion Queen", Ellen Chapman (who later married Bostock), was soon working the cages at Wombwell's. Both of these women were successors to an original "Lion Queen" who was touring with Hilton's as early as 1839. On the other hand, another correspondent recognised the menagerie as having a germ of edification and constituting a balance against the less salubrious entertainment that might otherwise beguile the working man and his family. While another reported that there were fewer cases of drunkenness reported in Wick when the menagerie came. Even at this early stage there seems to have been some reform in the menageries and they may as they became really big businesses (we have seen how much exotic animals cost) have acquired more and more of an air of respectability – as early as 1854 the *Times* published a nostalgic feature on "The Old Menageries". Certainly the following extract from the *Dundee, Perth and Cupar Advertiser* for 4th May 1858 shows how the menageries were starting to look like a relic of an earlier time although they still had a long life ahead of them:

> Manders's Menagerie. – On Thursday last we had a visit by the way of a menagerie, an event of rare occurrence now-a-days in our town. At twelve o'clock noon their band, an excellent one, driven in a beautiful car, paraded the town, playing favourite Scottish airs. This done, and after a short interval, the place was thrown open for admission, but few entered as it rained very heavily, the continuation of which prevented many country folks from coming to see it. However, towards night, owing to the stoppage of the rain, and we may also mention as stronger incentive, namely a lower charge of admission, great numbers visited the exhibition. This collection, though not very extensive, embraced some of the best specimens of natural history we ever recollect seeing, those especially worthy of notice being the lions, some ten or twelve in number. The principal attraction was "Maccomo" an African by birth, whose daring and cool performances in the lions' cage startled all and alarmed many.

As the century drew on the menageries became more like travelling zoos and less like circuses and, as we will see, the zoos were the main site where exotic animals met the Victorian reform of popular culture.

Sensational deaths of lion tamers or other handlers were matched by numerous accounts of mauled spectators – it is surprising there weren't more as Wombwell's longest serving lion tamer, a man called Manchester Jack, who ended his life in 1865 peaceably keeping a pub in Taunton, used to take people into the big cats' cages for an extra 6d (2.5p). Drunkenness often played a part in these accidents – the African lion tamer Alexander Young was drunk when he had a close call with his lions – as it did in the case of an assault on one of Wombwell's gazelles when a drunk twisted one of its horns off and tried to steal it. Escaped animals could be quite harmless such as the tapir which terrorised Rochdale (note that such a rare animal as a tapir was in the menagerie) or the elephant which broke into a pub in Holywell and made free with the contents of the cellar. But there were more exciting

THE TRAGIC DEATH OF THE LION QUEEN

incidents such as the two polar bears who broke free from Hilton's menagerie in February 1851 and rampaged through Liverpool city centre, where one ate a dog; or the bizarre incident of the Scottish farmer who was walking home from the menagerie when he suddenly found himself in the folds of a boa constrictor. Fortunately he was carrying an axe. In 1842, Wombwell's menagerie was at Croydon Fair and every day the elephant was taken for a walk into town and bought a bun at a local confectioner's. It so enjoyed this treat that at 3 a.m. one morning it pushed its way out of its cage and went into town on its own where it smashed the confectioner's windows and helped itself. It sometimes feels that an escapee lurked behind every tree in Victorian England but such animals could also be the subject of mistaken identity. For example, fears that the Russians had invaded were apparently provoked by the bear in Wombwell's menagerie while a shadowy figure that stalked the streets of Budleigh Salterton at night and terrified the locals was shot by a gamekeeper and proved to be a kangaroo.

We have already seen how "the tiger that swallowed the boy" became a star attraction and how the menageries talked up the dangers of their stock.

The following anecdote eloquently shows the attitude of some menager-ists to accidents. Frank Buckland was out looking at the salmon fisheries near Taunton with the zoologist Abraham Bartlett when they came across a menagerie and, of course, couldn't resist going in. A chief attraction was a show called "The Dwarf and the Wild Beasts" which consisted of a dwarf locked in a cage with a wolf and three bears. The dwarf got the bears to jump through a hoop but the wolf simply slunk along after him snarling nastily. Buckland spoke to him afterwards and he admitted that "I'm a bit afeard on him, he follows me about close like and has nipped me twice." Buckland thought it only a matter of time before the wolf went for the dwarf and the bears finished him off and he mentioned this anxiety to the menagerie's proprietor. He got a remarkable answer: "Shouldn't wonder at all, sir, if it did happen: but look here, sir, what a fine advertisement it would make!"

Menageries are an interesting case for the study of crime and society in Victorian England. The word menagerie is often used pejoratively to describe a riotous scene in the slums for example. It is also not uncom-monly used of the House of Commons or of politicians in general and when Lord Derby was attempting to form a government an opposition member shouted that he was surprised that he (Derby) had been so quick to sell his father's menagerie as he was now collecting one of his own. Menageries were undoubtedly crime scenes and associated with disorder but, at the same time, they hovered on a boundary between the genuinely popular entertainments that were in the eyes of many of the respectable classes (but not the Royal family) always a seat of viciousness and the increasing reform and gentrifica-tion of selected forms of these entertainments which is such a major feature of the Victorian period. The problem was that although you could stop the working man from drinking you couldn't stop the tiger from biting.

But although the menageries appear to be sites of disorder from one perspective, the evidence for their being an entirely disreputable form of enter-tainment is simply not there, whatever their reputation. We have seen that the customer base was, in fact, distributed from the poorest charity children to the Queen herself and that admission fees at the top end were not negli-gible. The owners of the most successful menageries claimed, not entirely without justification, to be naturalists in their own right and to be offering an educational service similar to that provided by the zoos. Wombwell even donated dead animals to the Saffron Walden Natural History Museum. Sometimes, the menageries were responsible for bringing new animals into the country and thus adding to the stock of zoological knowledge. In 1829, for example, Wombwell exhibited the first North American bison to be seen in Britain and subsequently sold them to Regent's Park. Records of animal longevity suggest that animals were well-treated by the standards of the day and, given the large investment a menagerie required, it would have been a poor businessman who neglected his stock. Even so, Thomas Frost remarked on the difficulty of keeping animals fit when they were on the road and the superiority of zoos when it came to welfare and accommodation. And there are enough records of prosecutions for cruelty to suggest that the training side of the business doesn't bear much inspection. The more respectable zoos learned a great deal from menageries as they developed their own business model. But, ultimately, I think the menageries are found guilty by association with the fairs. But without the fairs they would never have prospered to the extent they did or lasted so long. And it is clear that if you wanted to see an exotic animal in Victorian England a menagerie was the most likely place that you would go to fulfil your desire.

CHAPTER FOUR

Circus and Spectacle - A Playful Lion is a Terrible Thing

On Thursday May 3rd 1888 drinkers in pubs clustering round Hull's Alexandra dock became aware of a rumbling sound. The sound got louder and louder and they also began to pick out snorts, cries and whoops. For those of courageous disposition the curiosity to see what was causing this commotion was overwhelming and those who braved going outside were treated to the wonderful sight of a stampeding herd of about fifteen fully grown North American bison tearing full throttle down the Hedon Road and pursued by a band of increasingly agitated cowboys and Indians displaying that heady mixture of anxiety and glee that you see when removal men drop a grand piano. Buffalo Bill's Wild West Show was in town and things had not started well.

The Wild West Show was not really a vehicle for the display of exotic animals but it is a good starting point for this discussion of the Victorian circus as it contained, albeit in a rather specialised form, most of the ingredients of a typical circus and had much the same clientele. The Wild West Show was, predominantly, a horse show with spectacle and ethnographic curiosity thrown in. One of the highlights was the buffalo hunt where the herd which travelled with the show was stampeded round the ring with Buffalo Bill himself — never known as Bison Bill — pretending to hunt them down by firing blank cartridges. The bison were billed as "The last of the only known native herd" but that was far from the truth although men like Colonel Cody had certainly thinned their numbers dramatically. Not by riding them down and running the risk of being trampled as in the Wild West Show but by picking them off with state-of-the-art rifles at a range of over a mile away, a distance so great that the animals could not actually hear the gunshots and so were not scared off by the noise. Even so the hunting scene caused some anxiety in England and in 1887 the RSPCA investigated the animals' treatment and welfare – it appears they found nothing amiss.

The bison were the only part of the show that qualifies as an exotic animal display. There is always when dealing with zoos and circuses in the Victorian period the anxiety that the indigenous peoples who often featured in both were thought of as exotic creatures in some way. In fact, many of the Native Americans who travelled with Buffalo Bill were technically prisoners of war and the show was a convenient mobile prison for the United States Army. A rival Wild West Show, Miss Viola Clemmons's Company, actually advertised that its "full-blooded Sioux Indians" were "the only ones in this country excepting those held by Colonel W. F. Cody ("Buffalo Bill") as prisoners of war" and when the Ghost Dance movement started back in the USA many of Bill's company (those who were not prisoners of war) wanted to go home to join it.

The Wild West Show was supremely popular and made several tours of England, the last being just outside our period in 1903 and 1904 where the show toured Lincolnshire for the first time. Queen Victoria was a keen patron, as was the Prince of Wales, and as the show developed an English clientele it included customised material such as retired soldiers of the Lancers and Cossacks re-enacting the Charge of the Light Brigade. There were also Mexicans, Japanese Samurai, an oriental scene in which Arabs kidnapped and entertained Europeans until they were ransomed and, later, a re-enactment of scenes from the Boxer Rising. The attractions of the Wild West Show were the exotic displays as well as the virtuosic horsemanship and the remarkable shooting of Annie Oakley.

The success of Buffalo Bill's Wild West Show was briefly matched by Frank E. Fillis's Savage South Africa Show which performed as part of the Greater Britain Exhibition at Earls Court in 1899 and then moved on to Salford, Liverpool, Blackpool and Leeds before closing due to mounting losses in 1900. On the one hand, Savage South Africa, was a pale imitation of the Buffalo Bill formula which Fillis had noted as a good brand that he could copy. (Fillis had significant theatrical interests in South Africa and

SAVAGE SOUTH AFRICA

his wife had cut her teeth as a human cannon ball but was now part of a more genteel equestrienne display: my guess is that she quit the artillery business in 1893 after her loader, Monsieur Mayol, blew himself up during a performance in Melbourne.) On the other hand, it was a timely reconstruction of the stirring events of the Second South African War which was then raging and none too successfully from the British point of view. In this sense it was a throwback to the gigantic historical reconstructions of earlier in the century. Fillis's troupe included between 200 and 500 Zulus, Matabeles, Basutos, Hottentots, Swazis and Malays (accounts vary), ten Boer families, various members of the Cape Town Rifles, the South African Police and the Bechuanaland Police, 400 Basuto ponies, and eighty bucks together with seven lions, eight tigers (in South Africa?) and six elephants. Fillis had had some experience of staging historical spectaculars – in 1884 he was running a reconstruction of the Sudan war featuring the battles of El Teb and Tamaieb as part of his show in Cape Town – so although he was cashing in on the vogue for Buffalo Bill he was by no means a mere imitator. One of Fillis's star performers was an American known as Texas Jack who went to South Africa after the tour of England and started Texas Jack's Wild West Show there to some acclaim.

There are two early films of Savage South Africa. One shows a group of Zulus dancing on Southampton docks on the day or very near the day when the show arrived in England.

The other is called "Savage South Africa – attack and repulse" and shows one of the reconstructions that were part of the show. In this case a skirmish between British and Matabele soldiers. Indeed one of the stars of the show was Prince Peter Lobengula who claimed, probably truthfully, be the son of the great Matabele leader King Lobengula. He stayed in England after the end of the South Africa show after being involved in a scandal concerning his desire to marry an English woman called Kitty Jewell who enjoyed a significant five minutes of fame in the popular press. He eventually married an Irish woman and became a coal miner in Salford where he died in 1913. Oddly enough there is a legend that King Cetewayo of the Zulus also became a coal miner and died in Cardiff although his actual death in Zululand in 1884 is well attested so maybe this is a conflation with Peter Lobengula's story. Cetewayo visited London in 1882 and made several well-publicised visits to the zoo where crowds turned out to see him (as they did wherever he went) and there is an uneasy sense that he temporarily became part of the exhibition.

But the Lobengula scandal does demonstrate the nature of the Show – which appears to have consisted partly of set piece spectacle and partly of a "Kaffir Kraal" where visitors could wander through an African landscape and meet the locals. This caused great anxiety. *The Times* thought the show was a "capital circus performance" but did point out that not everyone would think that the idea of bringing over "large numbers of natives to be stared at and to take their chance of being demoralized in such strange and unedifying surroundings" was an especially good one and the case was not helped by Fillis's tactic of displaying his African employees at six pence (2.5p) a look to raise money for their accommodation. The Aborigines' Protection Society and others, including the influential Joseph Chamberlain (one forgets that the public voice in Imperial England was by no means univocal), condemned the show outright.

Others objected not so much to the display of native flesh in demoralising circumstances as to the indecent erotic potential of such a display especially as white women were allowed to visit the men's huts in the Kaffir Kraal. In South Africa itself the opposition to the show was explicitly concerned that exposure to white vice would corrupt the participants. Reading the numerous newspaper reports of the time it is clear that the Savage South Africa show touched some very raw nerves by bringing together issues of racial superiority (not helped by the Fillis's own advertisements in South Africa for "young Afrikander girls good looking and slightly coloured"), the fear of miscegenation, and the awkward vulnerability that the whole experience of the South African War had exposed in the Imperial world view. The Kraal was eventually ordered to close to women to prevent outbreaks of public immorality and this was what probably caused the show to lose its main revenue potential.

Round the reconstructions circulated the animals which must have been displayed in some form of associated menagerie as well as being used as picturesque props for the Kraal tableaux. Fillis was the first circus proprietor in South Africa to append a menagerie to the usual diet of equestrian and acrobatic acts – in 1888 his posters announced "The Lions! The Lions!" – so it is highly likely that he repeated this winning formula for Savage South Africa. Fillis toured his circus to Australia, New Zealand as well as India, China, Ceylon, the Straits Settlements and Java and these touring shows included the menagerie which by the 1890s was being incorporated into the circus via performing lions, tigers and elephants. In 1893 the show was in Sydney and Melbourne and in 1894 it was touring New Zealand where the lions and tigers in particular made an impression in Auckland (where they had toured before) and the menagerie included cheetahs, pumas, leopards, wolves, foxes, bears, monkeys and an orangutan.

So not only were exotic animals appearing in the circus in increasing numbers: they were touring the Empire and beyond. For example, Fitzgerald's circus which was operating in New Zealand in the late 1890s had, *inter alia*, an elephant who rode a giant tricycle while a lion balanced on its back. There were many circuses in Australia. Most consisted almost exclusively of traditional equestrian and acrobatic acts but some did include menageries and performing animals. Madame Woodyear's Circus and Great London Equescuriculum, which was in Brisbane in 1886, had a kind of boxing booth where you could wrestle a Russian bear – according to my cousin Taiaiake Alfred (Mohawk elder, Professor of Political Science and former US Marine) a similar facility existed about thirty years ago near Camp Lejeune in North

Carolina, but I doubt if the bears there were Russian (unless they were *spetsnaʒ* infiltrators). Chiarini's Royal Italian Circus had some real rarities – alongside the usual zebras and tigers – it had a performing bison and a troupe of performing South American guanacos. Cooper, Bailey and Co came over from the USA in 1876 and toured Australia with a massive menagerie which included elephants, giraffes, jaguars, leopards, bears, lions, tigers (including "Brazilian tigers", whatever they were), monkeys, zebras, a hippopotamus and a colony of Alaskan sea lions. This was the first time that many of these animals had been seen in Australia.

I have seen a report that a Savage Australia show was touring England in 1899 but I have not been able to find any source in a contemporary newspaper or magazine which confirms this although there were two groups of indigenous Australians from Queensland touring the world (including London, Belfast and Dublin) in the 1880s and 1890s. Although Australia was featured in many colonial exhibitions (usually as a place of plentiful production and agricultural abundance) indigenous people featured only sporadically as ethnographic exhibits from the 1870s onwards. None of these shows seemed to have featured Australian animals.

The Earl's Court Exhibition at which Savage South Africa made its debut was one of the many huge shows put on by the Hungarian impresario Imre Karalfy. Karalfy worked with Barnum on massive historical spectaculars depicting, among other things, Columbus's Discovery of America and when he moved to Britain he took some of these with him. The scale of these shows can be gauged by the size of the descriptive programmes which were sold to the audience. The one for Columbus runs to thirty-five pages and, in addition to the dramatic proceedings, there were scores for the immense orchestras which provided a live accompaniment to the stirring doings in the auditorium. Karalfy's best loved spectacular was his recreation of Venice but his shows did partake of the circus as they included not only the predictable horses but also, in the case of a show like *Nero*, which had a long run on both sides of the Atlantic, camels and elephants. Karalfy's greatest achievement was the staging of the London Olympics in 1908 and his White City was the site not only of the games but many other Imperial shows. At Earl's Court, Karalfy staged exhibitions called "Empire of India", "India and Ceylon", "The Victorian Era", "The Universal Exhibition", "Greater Britain", "Woman's", "International", "The Military" and "Paris in London" some of which (the India and Ceylon exhibitions) included elephants and other exotic animals. At the inauguration of the "Colonial and Indian Exhibition" in 1886 the second verse of the national anthem was sung in Sanskrit. Much of the White City site eventually became the BBC's headquarters in London and the last permanent exhibition buildings were demolished only two years ago to make way for a Westfield shopping mall.

The large exhibitions featuring displays of exotic domestic life could also be reproduced at home through *tableaux vivants*. Queen Victoria was especially fond of these and many were staged for her enjoyment at Osborne House. These included *Queen of Sheba*, *Carmen* and *Elizabeth and Raleigh* but there were also events which mirrored the great public exhibitions. These included *King of Egypt*, *Empire* and *An Indian Scene* where her various Indian servants enacted a tiger hunt using a propped-up tiger skin rug. So the Queen's great enjoyment of exotic animals was even reflected in the private entertainments devised by her household for her amusement. Indeed, when Prince Albert Victor came of age in January 1885 the various celebrations included a trip to Sanger's circus and a special entertainment from George Mann and his elephant Sherriff.

But the Victorian circus was only a marginal player in the exotic animal trade as, generally speaking, the displays concentrated heavily on equestrian acts. In this they were closely related to the "hippodramas" which constitute a now lost part of the entertainment landscape but were a crucial component of Victorian and slightly earlier spectacular theatre – although they are still popular in Australia. Certainly at the beginning of our period circuses were almost exclusively devoted to riding displays of varying degrees of daring and scale. Later, acrobatic shows begin to feature commonly. It is not until the 1880s that wild animal displays and, in particular, displays of performing wild animals start to become part of the staple diet of entertainment that people expected to find in a circus. This was probably a reaction to the enormous success of Barnum and Bailey's circus which did feature wild animals very heavily and which had first visited England to great acclaim in 1889–1890. This is not to say that wild animals had not featured in circuses before. Lion taming acts were common enough as were elephants and occasionally monkeys. The circus proprietor Edwin Hughes, for example, used to advertise his establishment by progressing through the town in a huge gilded carriage drawn by two elephants with Hughes himself dressed as a Rajah sitting in state in the midst of it all. George Sanger's wife took a star role in the parades which brought his circus into town: she led the procession dressed as Britannia with a lion (the gently disposed Nero) at her feet.

Before the 1880s it was sometimes difficult to tell the difference between a circus and a menagerie as many travelling circuses had a menagerie on display as part of the visitor experience even though the animals themselves did not perform. Similarly, most menageries put on displays which were the sort of thing that would later become circus acts and these were especially likely to feature a lion taming act. It could also be said that the early commercial zoos had many circus-like elements. If you went to the Surrey Zoological Gardens or Belle Vue you didn't only look at the animals you could also see massive spectacles, especially historical re-enactments such as the Battle of Waterloo or the Battle of the Alma (just as Buffalo Bill's show incorporated the Battle of Little Big Horn), which were of precisely the same kind offered by the bigger circuses. Similarly the distinction between the travelling menagerie and the static zoological gardens is reflected in a distinction between the smaller travelling circus with its lion tamer and troupes of bareback riders, acrobats – such as the famous rope dancer and equestrian Pablo Fanque who became a circus entrepreneur in his own right and whose nephew (also working under the name Pablo Fanque) toured Australia and New Zealand with an acrobatic circus in the 1850s and 1860s – and performing dogs and the huge fixed amphitheatre circuses such as what would eventually become Astley's Royal Amphitheatre and which was built at Lambeth and opened as early as 1768 with the first menagerie to be associated with a circus opening there in 1838. By 1840 this menagerie had started to provide animal acts such as that of "Carter the Lion King" who went up in a hot air balloon accompanied by a leopard.

As the nineteenth century wore on, travelling circuses such as Cooke's and Sanger's increased in size and, like the menageries, required significant numbers of purpose-built vehicles as well as draft animals to move around the country. When they rolled into town they would usually hitch a couple of elephants or a couple of dozen Shetland ponies to the wagons but otherwise they used standard horse power. The Sanger brothers took over Astley's amphitheatre in 1871 and gradually incorporated more exotic animal displays to replace the hippodramas presented by their predecessor Cooke (which included Shakespeare plays acted on horseback). One of these shows included a cast of 500 humans and fifty-two horses in the traditional hippodrama style but then added fifteen elephants, nine camels, and two lions prudently kept on leads (the production of *Nero* at the Hippodrome de L'Étoile in Paris in the 1850s had Christians being thrown to lions who were kept in artfully concealed cages) alongside a veritable Noah's

ASTLEY'S.—MR. PABLO FANQUE, AND HIS TRAINED STEED.

PABLO FANQUE

ark of ostriches, emus, pelicans, kangaroos, reindeer, hog deer, acis deer, brahma bulls, chamois and moufflons. Sanger also had a pleasing taste for the downright silly: one of his shows included goldfish that pushed boats around a little tank; another advertised the preposterous wonders of a tame oyster. James Myer seems to have been the first circus entrepreneur to use his menagerie to develop large-scale animal acts (rather than just a couple of elephants wandering round the ring or a lion tamer) and from the 1870s his show included a troupe of elephants and an act with seven lions but even this didn't stave off bankruptcy and Myer sold up in 1887 with his star elephant ("Blind Bill") and six remaining lions all going to John Cooper his head trainer.

Circuses travelling the country in the nineteenth century included Adams's, Bannister and West's, Barrington's Great Model, Batty's, Broekman's (a specialist dog and monkey circus), Clarke's, Cooke's, Franconi's, the French American, Ginnett's, Howe and Cushing's, Hengler's, Hughes's, Hutchinson and Tayleure's. Keith's, Myer's, the New American, Newsome's Alhambra, Newsome's Grand, the Olympic, Quaglini's, Sands's, Sanger's, Saunders's and Wieland's. This is by no means a complete list but gives some idea of the scale of the industry and therefore the number of animals which, at any one time, must have been travelling the roads and stiffly going through their routines in the fixed arenas or in large tents.

In 1900 the Christmas show at the Crystal palace featured Beketiff's Russian Circus with elephants, bears and four performing cats. It was a sign of the times that in another part of the building you could go to the pantomime but not as a live show: they had a cinematograph. At the end of the period the cinematograph became a supplement to the menageries: Hancock's "Living Pictures and Menagerie" which was originally set up by the lion tamer Richard Dooner and "Crecraft's Wild Beast and Living Pictures" were especially noteworthy – in the latter case not least because its proprietor Elizabeth Crecraft kept the show going until she was 92 years old (she died in 1918 aged 98). In 1903 (so slightly outside our period but included here as it is such a notable example of an exotic animal on a widely-shown film) Thomas Edison commissioned *Electrocuting an Elephant*. This shows the execution of a circus elephant called Topsy who had killed three people. The American SPCA refused to allow her to be hanged (which, astonishingly, was the original plan) so Edison stepped in and arranged her electrocution as a way of advertising the dangers of Tesla's alternating current system which was the rival to his direct current in the struggle to gain a monopoly in the power supply industry. The film makes gruesome viewing.

Reading contemporary newspaper accounts one is struck by the number of disasters that took place at circuses. In 1848 for example Pablo Fanque's wife was killed when a permanent circus building originally built for Hengler's collapsed. There are numerous examples of fire. Batty's went up in 1839, Cooke's in 1842 (not for the first time) and these were by no means the only ones. In pretty much every case the circus soon recovered and was sometimes burned down again (Hengler's was destroyed several times). Most famously Barnum's burned down in 1873 with the loss of many animals. Newspapers reported the bravery of a lion who roared to the last and the philosophical deportment of the elephants who meekly knelt to await their terrible fate. In addition there were accidents caused by escaping animals and the prurient risk of a lion tamer being eaten by his or her charges (which happened surprisingly frequently). In February 1888 eight wolves got out of their cage at Sanger's circus. These were finally subdued by the collective efforts of the circus's fire man, the lion tamer John Humphreys, Mr Oliver the circus deputy manager and a character called Alpine Charley who was a wolf trainer. The wolves managed to kill a horse but were finally barricaded in and a new cage was made. It appears that the wolves were deliberately released by two men who had been sacked earlier in the day. Five parrots died of fright. Not all these incidents resulted in a bad ending. When Batty's circus was visiting Ireland in 1872 a camel got out during their stay in Cork. It made its way down Great St George's Street and into the house of Jeremiah Desmond, a labourer. Desmond was happily sitting on the front step of his house preparing food for his pig when he was suddenly crushed against the door jamb by "a queer thing" which proved to be Batty's camel. Desmond sued Batty for personal injury and Mr Hayes the examining magistrate now asked him why the camel didn't it come any further into the house to which Desmond answered to the huge enjoyment of the court: "God almighty, sir, the hump." Desmond claimed £15 in damages but was awarded three which must have been a lot of money to a labourer in late-nineteenth-century Cork.

There were also individual acts. At the top end of the scale was the American lion tamer Isaac Van Amburgh. He had started his career as a cage cleaner in a menagerie and had gradually acquired his own travelling collection enlivened by his own feats with the big cats. He first appeared in London in 1838, having first tried out his full act in the United States in 1833, and performed at Drury Lane in 1839 where he was a sensation. Queen Victoria patronised the act and loved it. She went six times and even asked for a special show involving feeding time – Van Amburgh starved his animals for thirty-six hours previously to make sure she got a really good spectacle. All this guaranteed Van Amburgh his continued success on both sides of the Atlantic for the patrician American republicans, then as now, liked nothing better than royal approval. What Van Amburgh's act was designed to display was the mastery of men over brute animals (even noble animals like big cats) and, dressed the clothes of a Roman from antiquity with the title, "the brute conqueror of Pompeii", he would stroll around in cage full of lions, leopards and tigers demonstrating who was boss. To rub in the point and make the big cats seem even more subdued he would carry a lamb around with him and even let it frisk (if it had the nerve to do it) around the cage. His other act involved him in more humble attire and presenting a tableau of himself as Daniel in the Lions' Den.

ISAAC VAN AMBURGH AND HIS ANIMALS

Van Amburgh's displays reinforced two things. The first was the right of dominion that man enjoyed by divine decree over the rest of sentient creation. The second was the dominion of western empires (it is not accident that van Amburgh dressed like a Roman) over other cultures. The Duke of Wellington got the idea immediately and had, in 1847, commissioned Land-seer's painting *Portrait of Mr Van Amburgh as He Apppeared with his Animals at the London Theatres* to hang in the drawing room at Apsley House with a special frame embellished with the verses from *Genesis* in which God gives the right of dominion to Man. This 1847 picture was Landseer's second treatment of Van Amburgh's act and it is worth comparing the two paintings for what they tell us about shifting attitudes to the display of wild animals and especially lions.

The first picture, *Isaac Van Amburgh and his Animals*, was produced in 1839 as a commission for Queen Victoria herself and it is still in the Royal Collection. The image shows Van Amburgh in his Roman clothing reclining in a cage with his lamb pressing close against him. A leopard is looking hungrily at the lamb, a huge lion is sitting peaceably and nobly behind him and a tiger (on whose head Van Amburgh is resting his hand) is snarling at a lioness. We the viewers are inside the cage with Van Amburgh and the animals and are part of the spectacle as through the bars we can see the audience depicted on an artificially small scale and peering somewhat anxiously and grimly at the events unfolding inside. Only one person, an African in western dress, appears uninterested and is looking away to the horizon – it is tempting to see in this a subtle and subdued comment on the likely attitude of the colonised to the coloniser. The picture is, nevertheless, designed as an accurate depiction of the kind of show the Queen would have seen and by situating the viewpoint inside the cage Landseer offers a reprise of the *frisson* the Queen must have enjoyed when she witnessed the savagery of the feeding. Equally, by placing the viewer in the cage Landseer enables him or her vicariously to participate in the act of domination depicted.

The Duke of Wellington's picture, which was completed in 1849, is a very different affair. Here Van Amburgh is in his Daniel costume and is adopting a melodramatic pose. He is pointing at a lion who is cringing in the corner with his back to Van Amburgh and is folding his front legs in front of him in an almost sulky attitude. A lioness and leopard look cowed. A tiger

PORTRAIT OF MR VAN AMBURGH

snarls and another leopard looks as if it might pounce. Van Amburgh looks decidedly nervous. This is not the picture of a confident performance. The animals look as if they are kept in check only by the threat of the whip in Van Amburgh's right hand, Van Amburgh looks far from at ease among the big cats, and the whole thing looks tawdry. We are now placed outside the cage and in the foreground are the debris of a day's enjoyment: discarded orange peel, a discarded nosegay, what looks like the remnants of a Roman triumphal crown. It feels as if the viewer is making his or her way home after a day's entertainment and the last act is desperately trying to drum up that last bit of custom. Tellingly a torn poster has blown against the bottom of the cage. It tells us that this is Van Amburgh's last appearance and informs us that next week the entertainment will be *The Taming of the Shrew*. It's surprising the Duke paid up but apparently he missed all the satire and bathos in this picture and saw it as an uncomplicated restatement of the Biblical right of dominion of man over the animals. But Landseer was clearly in satirical mode and *The Examiner* saw the point, saying that the image reduced the majesty of Divine will regarding dominion to such an extent that "any itinerant professor of dog dancing" could have been pictured to make the same point.

Van Ambergh did, however, have the respect of other lion tamers. A lengthy interview with the famous French lion tamer Bidel in 1887 mentioned him along with Charles and Martin as lion tamers who had lived to good old ages and died in their beds in contrast with Lucas or the Turk, Agop Shaninion, who were torn to pieces by their animals or Agop's widow Nouma Hawa (a female lion tamer not to be confused with Princess Nouma Hawa who toured with Barnum as "the smallest woman in the world") who at the time of the interview was in a lunatic asylum – but this must have been the shock of losing her husband as there are posters for her act dating from 1888. Other female lion tamers who were world famous and toured internationally at the same time were Claire Heliot and Ida Krone (who began her lion-taming career under the prosaic name of Miss Charles). A painting by the German artist Paul Meyerheim shows an exotically dressed woman with a parrot on her shoulder stroking a lion's mane while a lioness snarls and threatens. This has been proposed as a portrait of Heliot but as she was only fourteen at the time the painting was produced this seems unlikely.

One site which blended the thrills of the circus with spectacle and theatre was the Royal Aquarium and Winter Garden in Westminster. This will be briefly mentioned in another chapter for its display of whales and other rare aquatic mammals but as the attractions of the aquarium were plainly insufficient to keep the proprietors in profit they diversified and included several animal acts alongside the human performers. These included Pongo the gorilla (a rarity at that time) and one night's programme included alongside everything else Professor Wingfield's dogs, a Wonderful Donkey and Sam Lockhart's Six Marvellous Performing Elephants. In 1892 Professor Landermann exhibited his boxing kangaroo there and this proved extremely popular for a season – Landermann (as Lindemann) had previously had a good career managing a kangaroo called "Fighting Jack" in Australia. In 1893 a Louis Wain drawing published in *The Sketch* showed the Aquarium's boxing dogs, balancing goats, and leopard or panther taming act. Other theatres also included animal acts – for example the celebrated tightrope walking Blondin Donkey which performed in various music halls and at Drury Lane theatre in 1885 – but only the Royal Aquarium had kangaroos, gorillas and manatees.

There were star human performers like Pablo Fanque and Nouma Hawa but some circus animals developed their own followings and were characters in their own right. For example, Sanger had a favourite elephant called Charlie and he grew to be the largest elephant ever seen in captivity in England. Like many elephants Charlie didn't manage to last out his captivity and was eventually put down after killing a circus carpenter – although Myer's Blind Bill killed two keepers. Even more famous was the lion Wallace. Wallace was born in Edinburgh in 1812 and lived his life in Wombwell's menagerie together with another favourite lion, Nero, whom Wombwell had acquired from Polito who had exhibited him at both the Exeter Exchange and the Tower of London. Wallace's most celebrated moment came in 1825 when Wombwell arranged for Nero to fight six dogs (in pairs) at Warwick. Although this sounds like a low event aimed at a large audience it was actually pretty exclusive and the surviving tickets – with a wonderful engraving of a lion with NERO! written below it – show an entry fee of one guinea (£1.05) and this suggests that the story that Wombwell was put up to it by two well-to-do gamblers is true. Apparently other tickets were priced at five guineas (£5.25) which suggests that a good deal of money changed hands that day. Nero was an easy-going animal and refused to fight even though he was badly bitten and bleeding so Wallace was brought in. He dealt with all the dogs in a few minutes. In 1827 he killed a man called John Wilson who pushed his arm through the bars of his cage. Wallace died in 1838 and can still be seen, stuffed, in Saffron Walden

Museum. Originally, he was mounted with one paw resting on a dog but he is now less controversially displayed prowling across a desert landscape. Wallace is an important specimen as he was, although born in Scotland, an example of the North African Barbary lion. After Wallace's death Wombwell bid on another lion called Wallace who had arrived in England in 1838 but he was outbid by Batty who paid £100 for him in the auction. Nero also lives on. Landseer produced a virtuoso chalk and charcoal drawing of him in 1820. In 1825, perhaps in celebration of his pacifism at Warwick (which led to the final banning of animal baiting in England) a fine Staffordshire figure with versions in both pearl ware and copper lustre was produced and when Wombwell died in 1850 a fine stone model of the lion (which was, by this time, essentially a pet) was carved and still rests above his grave in Highgate Cemetery.

Nero's own death in 1827 was sufficiently noteworthy to warrant a short obituary in the "Fashionable World" section of *The Morning Post*. Both Nero and Wallace have a literary afterlife. One of the early twentieth-century

GEORGE WOMBWELL'S GRAVE

American children's writer Richard Barnum's (a pseudonym for a number of ghost writers) most popular titles was *Nero the Circus Lion*, while Wallace features as the name of the lion in the English comedian Stanley Holloway's monologue *Albert and the Lion*. When Parker the lion died in America in 1879 the *Lancaster Gazette* thought the event worth recording as it gave its readers the chance to relive the moment when Parker – at that time being exhibited in London – dragged his keeper Crockett round his cage by the throat and nearly killed him.

Just as today circuses featuring animals are increasingly rare in the developed world due to public outcry about alleged animal cruelty there was by the mid nineteenth century some concern over the treatment of caged animals in zoos and spectacles and especially concerns over what were thought of as the higher animals – which certainly included lions and tigers. Even the Zoological Society of London, which would have prided itself with some reason on the highest and most modern standards of animal care, came in for criticism in Dickens' *Household Words*. In 1871 Batty was prosecuted and fined thirty shillings with ten shillings costs for allowing twelve horses to develop bleeding sores on their shoulders.

The circus sometimes came to the zoo. We will see in a later chapter how some private zoos survived through displaying animals in a manner which blurred the distinction between the zoo and the circus – as the travelling menageries had always done. We have also seen how Forepaugh tried to hoax the public with a whitewashed elephant. This was in response to a stunt by Barnum who, in early 1884, had bought a white elephant called Toung Taloung from the King of Burma (he claimed for £40,000 although the sum is likely to have been very much lower than that, perhaps no more than £150). This animal was exhibited at Regent's Park between January and March 1884. The animal was displayed as an important zoological specimen and although there was a good deal of disappointment in the colour – it was not white but a very pale grey with pink blotches – among the general public who came in extra numbers to see it the zoo's professional naturalists were satisfied as they knew that this was a colour of elephant that, while not uncommon in Thailand or Burma, had not often, if ever, been seen in England. Barnum made a great thing of the animal and played on the myths that surround the idea of the white elephant. On 26th and 27th January he had some oriental-looking men dress up as Burmese Buddhist priests and perform a service of veneration in the elephant's enclosure. This drew horrified protests from

Orientalist scholars and the zoo authorities asked Barnum not to repeat the show. They were, of course, compromised as the ceremony had drawn in an unusual number of paying customers. When the elephant left for New York it appeared to have become paler and Pears' soap put out an advertisement showing a white elephant being scrubbed clean. Although London Zoo tried to maintain itself as a pure site of scientific inquiry and recreation this was not, as we will see in the next chapter, the only time that it allowed itself to ensure that its commercial viability would be protected even at the expense of its higher reputation.

CHAPTER FIVE

Zoological Gardens -
I Have Known Human
Lovers of the Wombat

In the mid 1850s there were few things more pleasant for a gentleman artist and a lady poet to do than visit the wombat in London Zoo. As the Zoo's own Guidebook said:

> A portion of the Porcupine Inclosure is appropriated to a pair of very singular Marsupial Animals from Tasmania, which, for the first time on record, bred here in 1856.

Wombats had been kept in the zoo since 1830 so they were not an unfamiliar sight but to get a breeding pair was a real achievement and it was not only the managers of the zoo who were pleased. The public was delighted.

So let us imagine a day in 1857, perhaps the same day that in a less salubrious part of London a Bengal tiger had picked up the boy John Wade who was then fearlessly rescued by Charles Jamrach, and let us go to the wombat enclosure in London Zoo. First we need to find the monkey house and we can stop there for a while and be amused by the antics of the inmates. Or maybe we will be shocked by their glum inactivity and begin to think, as Gustave Doré plainly thought when he engraved them showing the view from inside the cage with the monkeys clustered together like the inmates of an asylum while indistinct faces float like balloons on the other side of their barred cage, that there is something wrong that these creatures, so uncomfortably like us, should be so imprisoned. Once we have had enough of the monkeys we must follow the path towards the Falcon Aviary and before we arrive there we will see the wombats. They are easy enough to find.

Chapter Five

A bewhiskered gentleman who, as we can see when he removes his hat to acknowledge an acquaintance, is prematurely balding, is approaching with a lady in sober dress and with a pinched face. We imagine her to look like a woman from one of the romances by the slightly shocking new American writer Nathaniel Hawthorne which we are reading with some delighted guilt. They pause and look at the wombat. "Oh look at that delightful object!" exclaims the woman.

The gentleman is William Rossetti. He is, in no particular order, a literary scholar, a tax inspector, an art critic, a part-time soldier, a journalist, an editor, and a founding member of the Pre-Raphaelite Brotherhood. Today he is just a wombat fancier enjoying a day out away from the Inland Revenue Board where he fast rising through the ranks. The lady is his sister Christina Rossetti who has yet to enjoy her greatest success but is beginning to build an impressive reputation among those who know about and care about poetry. Missing from this family party is the well-known artist Dante Gabriel Rossetti. Like his brother and sister he is a frequent visitor to the zoo (it is convenient to their family home in Charlotte Street) but he hasn't yet seen the wombats. After this visit William reminisced that:

> I soon instructed my brother what part of the Zoological Gardens he should go in order to contemplate the form and proportions of the wombat: he, I surmise, afterwards put Burne-Jones up to the same quest.

Dante Gabriel became the most dedicated devotee of wombats and later owned two although, arguably, Burne-Jones was the more obsessive with wombats featuring in the imaginative world of his delightful cartoons on and off over many years. But once he had caught the wombat bug from William and Christina Dante Gabriel would often arrange to meet his friends at "the wombat's lair"

The various descriptions that the Rossetti circle have left us of the wombats in London Zoo tell us quite a lot about the atmosphere and nature of that establishment in the middle of the nineteenth century. A letter of 18th August 1858 from Christina to William for example tells us of one visit to the zoo in which:

> ...the blind wombat and the neighbouring porcupine broke forth

into short-lived hostilities, but apparently without permanent results.

So one of the wombats was blind (very probably the effect of the sarcoptic manage which is endemic in certain populations of Tasmanian wombats) but still blundering around its enclosure. In addition, the strategy of keeping wombats and porcupines together seems not have been considered in the light of their likely compatibility when it came to sharing territory. Sometime later the minor Pre-Raphaelite painter Val Prinsep recalled a visit to see the wombats in the company of Dante Gabriel Rossetti:

> I made the acquaintance of this quadruped later, in company with Rossetti himself, who prodded the beast with his stick, and roared with laughter at his movement.

So visitors could tease the animals and get too close to them. As a child Christina had been bitten by a peccary – so annoying the animals was clearly a family habit.

We will leave the Rossettis looking at wombats now and start to reflect on what their visit tells us and about what the zoo was for, how it came into being and what kinds of experience of exotic animals it might have offered. We will also look at other zoos in England and some further afield. In this chapter much familiar material will be addressed – the history of London Zoo has been well written several times for example and there are excellent general works on the formation of zoological gardens in Europe from antiquity to the present. For this reason the concentration of this chapter will be on some of the less familiar territory while still trying to ensure that as comprehensive a picture as possible is presented of the opportunities that zoos offered to see and experience exotic animals.

London Zoo – or to give it its proper name the Zoological Gardens of the Zoological Society of London – came into being, as so many good things do, as the result of a terrible disaster.

In February 1824 Sir Thomas Stamford Raffles, founder of Singapore and highly respected Imperial administrator, was sailing home to England on the *Fame*. On board he had his wife, his books, his collections of natural and ethnographic curiosities and a sizeable menagerie of exotic animals including a tapir, a leopard and some pheasants. There was, as Raffles himself said of this "perfect Noah's Ark", "scarcely an unknown animal in Sumatra, whether bird, mammal or fish, that we did not have on board." Only a few hours out and the ship caught fire and went down. Everything was lost but Sir Stamford and Lady Raffles got away in a life boat so, as he said with creditable stoicism, "we must not complain." It took another three months to equip another ship for the voyage home and, in that time, Raffles, now freed from official duties, collected another private zoo – a very sizeable one too as the catalogue of those which eventually found their way to the Zoological Gardens in London ran to over sixty pages (including birds and insects) – which reached home safely. Lady Raffles's book about her husband's achievements the *Memoir of the Life and Public Services of Sir Thomas Stamford Raffles* makes many references to the animals that he kept during his posting to Malaysia including the comment, from one of Raffles's own letters that "our house is on one side a perfect menagerie, on another a perfect flora, here a pile of stones; there, a collection of sea-weeds, shells etc." Raffles's scholarship was sufficient for him to be valued as a contributor to the prestigious *Transactions* of the Linnaean Society. However, he was more than an academic zoologist, botanist and conchologist. He also liked the animals. Here he is speaking of his pet sun bear:

> He was brought up in the nursery with the children; and when admitted to my table…gave a proof of his taste by refusing to eat any fruit but mangosteen or to drink any wine but champagne. The only time I ever saw him out of humour was an occasion when no champagne was forthcoming.

A pair of orangutans wandered round the residence in full European costume. Although we are dealing here with the 1820s and are therefore outside of the period of interest for this book Raffles offers an interesting case study as in his career and his constellation of interests we can see coming together many of the themes and patterns we have already encountered.

As one of the founders of the British Empire, Raffles clearly understood his role as going far beyond the development of the economic and political advantages that flowed from colonisation and settlement. He was concerned to understand the new world in which he found himself and to classify and then communicate that knowledge to the home audience. He also wanted to promote the study of the natural world in the colonies themselves and re-established the Batavian Society as well as making various visits to the various learned societies and their collections in India. In addition, we see what we saw in our treatment of Jamrach's business that the combination of exotic animals, curiosities and shells offered a natural collection to anyone with Raffles's interests and sense of duty. However, while other colonial administrators were developing their collections in order to foster their own obsessions, advantage or profit, Raffles seems to have been entirely disinterested and concerned solely with the pursuit of knowledge and the promotion of the benefits of the Imperial project. In speaking of the loss of his collection and papers Raffles made a very explicit connection between Imperialism and science which shows very clearly some of the things that might have motivated the founders of the London Zoo:

> It has always appeared to me, that the value of these countries [modern Malaysia and Singapore] was to be traced rather through the means of their natural history, than in the dark recesses of Dutch diplomacy and intrigue; and I accordingly, at all times, felt disposed to give encouragement to those deserving men, who devote themselves to the pursuits of science.

So the physical mapping and taxonomy of territory, flora and fauna via the various disciplines of natural history and the natural sciences was, for Raffles, an extension of colonial politics and a way of gaining advantage over local rivals – in this case the Dutch. And we have already seen how directly linked the waxing and waning of Imperial fortunes could be when it came to the availability of exotic animals. In promoting the foundation of the zoo Raffles explicitly connected the beast shows of "Rome, at the period of her greatest splendour" with the desire to ensure that another Imperial capital offered "another, and a very different series of exhibitions, to the population of her metropolis; namely, animals brought from every part of the globe to be applied either to some useful purpose, or as objects of scientific research, not of vulgar admiration."

William Farquhar a predecessor and sometime colleague of Raffles as resident of Malacca (now Melaka) also kept a significant menagerie and had a wonderful series of illustrations made of them and other flora and fauna by local Chinese artists (as did Raffles for his collection but he used the French artist Briois as well as local painters). Farquhar and Raffles had a tense relationship and a final falling out, with Raffles clearly uneasy at Farquhar's claim to have been the true founder of Singapore. Farquhar was the first European to describe the Malaysian tapir but as he published his work in the transactions of the Bengal Asiatic Society, Raffles – who published in London – not only got his own article out first but actually appears to have tried to hinder the publication of Farquhar's piece which clearly predated his own. He didn't succeed and, in fact, the French zoologist Desmarest published the first article on the Malaysian tapir in 1819. This was heavily based on Farquhar's work which he properly acknowledged.

The idea of promoting Empire via science came to the fore in April 1826 when Raffles read a paper at a public meeting in which he recommended the formation of a Zoological Association. This was duly agreed and by May of the same year a Council of eighteen Fellows plus officers had agreed the new society's aims: which were to establish a zoological museum, a zoological library and a collection of live animals that would form the object of study and help to foster interest in the work of the society as more and more people saw them. Thus was London Zoo founded but it is not part of the scope of this book to dwell in detail on the politics of the subsequent years and the many twists and turns of policy and economic fortune which those founding fellows endured before the final opening of the Zoo in Regent's Park. What we must say is that by 1828 much building work was in progress under the supervision of the noted architect Decimus Burton. However, the construction of the permanent animal houses and enclosures proceeded at a slower pace than the arrival of the live animals and so the original collection (of 430 animals) was kept in mobile cages which were parked in Camden Town overnight and wheeled each day to Regent's Park no doubt to the delight of those who lived on the route and, one assumes, the occasional irritation of those who lived on the streets in which they were parked.

But why was it felt necessary to found a zoo which had these scientific and educational ambitions? As we have seen, there were plenty of ways to see or study exotic animals available to many people in England in the nineteenth century so why was it decided to develop a new one? There are several answers to this question.

One resides in national pride and the existence of what were clearly the forerunners of modern zoos in Vienna (the *Tiergarten Schönbrunn*, founded in 1752) and, especially, in Paris (the *Jardin des Plantes*, founded in 1793). These were an embarrassment to the English who felt that although their contributions to natural science through luminaries like Sir Joseph Banks far outshone what was done on the continent they as yet had no site by which to demonstrate their supremacy. Raffles himself had visited the Parisian *Jardin des Plantes* in 1817 and had been impressed by the way in which what had been the remnants of the old royal menagerie had been transformed into a scientific institution in which disciplined taxonomic and physiological study was adding to the sum of knowledge at a rate far in advance of what could be achieved by the random acquisition of an exotic specimen or a visit to a menagerie. In addition, as we saw in the case of Hagenbeck, the predominance of Britain as a world power at this time together with the shipping routes that were commonly used before the opening of the Suez Canal meant that an English facility would have huge advantages when it came to the collection and systematic organisation of the exotic animals themselves. So the zoo can be readily seen as another manifestation of Empire growing out of the specific circumstances that the Empire offered at this time. Sometimes these circumstances could be very specific indeed. For example, let's consider the two Afghan Boundary Commissions. As a result of the first, one officer brought home a beautiful Central Asian tiger and a group of Central Asian antelopes having secured passage from Khiva only by winning over the daughter of the senior Russian official there. So even exotic animals could be part of the Great Game played with the Russians on the North-West Frontier. As a result of the second, there was later the gift of two cheetah cubs, a snow leopard and another Asian tiger from the Nawab Mirzah Hassan Ali Khan.

Another answer resides in what is sometimes referred to as the reform of popular culture. Up until the later eighteenth century little notice had been taken of popular culture and, if it was noticed at all, it was noticed as crude, violent and probably a threat to public order. It worried John Locke for example. The Enlightenment changed all that and, increasingly, there was a desire – which was occasionally enacted through the statute books – to create a more civil society in which the benefits of culture and education would, whether the people liked it or not, come to hold more attraction than the gore of a bear baiting or a dog fight or the excitement of bare knuckle boxing. One French visitor to England in the eighteenth century noted that the English were addicted to excessive drinking, bad language, incredibly violent and disorderly sports, keeping inappropriately savage dogs and that they were extraordinarily tolerant of casual aggression and low level inter-personal violence on the street. As we have seen, one of the sites in which this anarchic combination found a rich expression was the travelling menagerie and the animals themselves seemed often to join the fray adding frolics of their own and other pieces of exotic mayhem.

Popular culture was, therefore, a ripe target for reform and it was reformed. There were attempts (which had gradual and varied success: on one occasion in Staffordshire the militia sent to shut down an especially disorderly bull running joined the bull runners) at suppressing animal baiting and festivals involving cruelty to animals; there were better provisions for public education and improvement, and things like temperance clubs were established. At the top end of the social scale the great public schools were reformed (a process described in the Victorian best seller *Tom Brown's Schooldays*) and became seats of learning and culture in which a gentlemanly pupil was marked more by his Christian piety, his sporting prowess and his good manners than by his capacity to drink a bottle of port in one go, to control and enjoy a harem of "bitches" in his dormitory or to kill another boy during a violent argument or in the course of a particularly sadistic bout of bullying.

Thus a pincer movement drove English culture towards a self-defined middle-class or upper-middle-class norm in which we find the qualities, for example that of understatement, that are often associated with Englishness. The game of cricket is a good case study of this shift. At this time, it began to be transformed. No longer was it primarily a gambling game in which local squires kept big-hitting batsmen and demonic fast bowlers in much the same way they kept jockeys and where matches could end (as did one between a team from Essex and a team from Kent) in a stabbing and a fire fight with muskets. From now on it was to be a genteel pursuit designed to inculcate discipline, fairness and manly intercourse between the classes. Just the qualities needed to be an officer setting a good example both to your men and to your native subjects. At this time, we also see the formation of the earliest philanthropic societies devoted to the protection of animals and the first legal moves to protect animals from excessive cruelty or exploitation.

Into this movement entered the zoo. Zoological gardens, it was hoped, would offer a space of education in which animals were to be viewed as scientific specimens, as proof of the coherent plan of the creator and as demonstrations of the breadth and benignity of Empire and not as wild curiosities or things to do tricks or only to be viewed in a context of the constant threat of danger and outrage. The zoo would offer what the menagerie could not and that was a polite space in which the benefits of civilisation and education would supersede the allures of the old popular culture and in which the working class and the lower middle class would learn from their betters (and, I suppose, from the animals) what it was to be a civil person at the centre of Empire.

By the end of the nineteenth century pretty much every European capital had a serious zoo as did the capitals of the Australian states, the major cities of India and what is now Pakistan and other imperial centres such as Hong Kong and Singapore. There were many zoos in the United States and also in the colonial capitals of other Empires such as Saigon and Jakarta. The worthies of the provincial towns of the British Isles couldn't sleep easy in their beds until their town had acquired a zoo and between the between the founding of London Zoo and the end of Queen Victoria's reign no fewer than twenty-nine zoos and aquaria came and went in all four countries of the then United Kingdom. Some, like Bristol still thrive, others, like Preston or Hull are now memories although traces often remain such as the Bear Castle which is still to be seen at Headingley and is the last remnant of the Leeds Zoological Garden or the stone slope down to the river at Cheltenham which was used to bathe the elephants which once lived in the short-lived (1838–1844) zoo there. Actually, Cheltenham has a persistent and odd connection with elephants. In 1934 some circus elephants rioted when passing Woodville's pet store which, they suspected, might harbour some tasty treats and in 1940 the Bertram Mills circus elephants visited to drink the spa waters in an effort to stave off their arthritis.

In London, however, the objective of using the zoo as a site of general education and improvement only slowly dawned on the founders of the Zoological Gardens and, initially, entrance to the Zoo was available only to Fellows of the Zoological Society (which received a Royal Charter in 1829) – these had paid a £3 joining fee and an annual subscription of £2 – and friends of Fellows. They could obtain a ticket from their friend and this gave day entrance only for one shilling (5p). These were high sums and the intention was clearly both to limit visiting to people who had committed to genuine scientific interest but also, crucially, to ensure that only the right sort of people gained entry. As a letter in *The Tatler* put it, the idea was "to prevent contamination of the Zoological Garden by the admission of the poorer classes of Society". The poorer classes would still have to depend for the moment on the less respectable thrills of the various menageries but, nevertheless, some 30,000 people visited the zoo in its first seven months which demonstrates the relatively large size of the elite target audience. It would not be until 1847 that the zoo finally threw open its gates to the paying public (i.e. you did not have to know member of the society but could get in at the door) at the reduced rate of sixpence (2.5p) on a Monday and a shilling for the rest of the week with Sundays being reserved for members only. Tickets were attractive items in themselves and showed an elephant, two monkeys, a zebra, two kangaroos, a Brahmin bull, a reindeer, an ostrich and various water birds. Amsterdam Zoo was founded in 1838 on a strictly members-only basis and with the same stiff subscription as Regent's Park but there the Zoo got round the problem of pent-up demand by having an annual "inexpensive month" where you could get in on an admission fee only (but even this was higher than working people could afford), by holding special events such as the display of two hippopotami in 1860, and through what we would now call an outreach programme offering free (but restricted) entry to teachers and pupils from 1862.

This opening up vastly increased numbers of visitors but it could not have initially done much to broaden the social mix as the entry price still represented a good deal of cash for a working man or woman especially if they then had to find sixpence for each of their children to get in with them. In addition early accounts of visitors and some early pictures suggests that even when the admission was strictly limited to members and their friends this did not, by any means, guarantee especially high standards of behaviour. We have already seen Dante Gabriel Rossetti poking the wombat with his stick but this was a pretty ordinary way of interacting with the animals in a zoo of this period. In fact, attempts were made to stop members taking their sticks and umbrellas into the gardens from as early as 1832 and this must surely have been to save the animals from unnecessary prodding. In June 1867, the Secretary was instructed to write to the Earl of Kimberley asking him not to smoke on the lawns and to comply with reasonable requests not to do so in future. But these were mild infringements. One of the great attractions of the zoo was the bear pit and keepers had concessions, according to seniority, to sell buns which visitors could then feed to the bears as they padded about in the pit or climbed the pole in the middle. One man dropped his hat into the bear pit and clambered down after it, compounding this rash decision by foolishly using a sleeping bear as a stepping stone. The startled bear grabbed him and had to be beaten off by the keepers. The other bears, frustrated of a promising afternoon's amusement with a new friend, tore up the hat in rage and then the man had the gall to try to charge the zoo for a new one. Another man – Walter Hamilton Goodfellow – went so far as to try to steal a bell bird. He was caught and fined £5 as well as being compelled to pay the zoo £10 for the value of the bird which was killed during this larcenous attempt. Other visitors to the zoo attempted fraudulent claims such as the old lady who tried to get compensation for a monkey-damaged hat – she had no success as the zoo had displayed clear notices saying that the management could not be responsible for hats stolen by monkeys – or the man who claimed to have been run over by an elephant but lost his case when witnesses could not place him and the elephant on the same stretch of pathway. Visitors in 1840 had the remarkable opportunity to watch an eleven foot long boa constrictor and a nine foot long boa constrictor begin to eat the same pigeon. This ended with the smaller snake being entirely consumed by the bigger one who then didn't eat for twenty-eight days. In another version of the story (the one presented above is from *The Times*, the other is the keeper Bartlett's account – surely the same thing didn't happen twice) the smaller snake was off its food and the bigger one having polished off a rabbit and three guinea pigs thought it would take advantage of its sluggish companion.

By the middle of the nineteenth century the zoo was a well-established feature of the capital and was a step forward in the way that Londoners and visitors could see and experience at first hand exotic animals when compared with the old fixed menageries. However, in its early days it had a rival in the form of Edward Cross's Surrey Zoological Gardens in Walworth. Cross set up this facility using the animals from his Exeter 'Change (or Royal) menagerie which had to be moved when its permanent home was demolished in 1829. This venerable institution had been based in the Strand since 1773 and under the proprietorship of Gilbert Pidcock, and then Stephen Polito, had grown to be a major, if depressing and somewhat noisome, attraction. The menagerie included lions, tigers, panthers, hyenas, leopards, jaguars, lynxes, porcupines, pelicans, cranes, gnus, ostriches, alpacas, llamas, kangaroos, emus, black swans, vultures, eagles, an orangutan, boa constrictors, a sloth, crocodiles and all manner of small mammals, monkeys and birds. It had housed the famous elephant Chunee who was put to death in 1826 after succumbing to *musth*. So when Cross set up the Surrey gardens he had a pretty good

---

*   A periodic condition in bull elephants, characterised by highly aggressive behaviour, accompanied by a large rise in reproductive hormones.

collection. Like the Regent's Park enterprise, the Surrey Zoological Gardens had a learned veneer, being formally the property of Cross's own *Surrey Literary, Scientific and Zoological Institution* (subsequently called the *Surrey Zoological and Botanical Institution*) which he founded, it appears, specifically as a customer for his animals and to which he sold them for £3,500.

As well as the zoo the gardens had the other forms of entertainment that a visitor would have expected to find in one of the popular pleasure gardens like Vauxhall or Cremorne. In fact, animal displays often formed an important part of the amusements available in a Victorian pleasure ground – we know, for example, from the record of Rossetti's activities as a collector that he bought at least some animals from "beast shows" at the Cremorne Gardens which were on the banks of the Thames more or less opposite his house in Chelsea; and in Cheltenham, that magnet for elephants, pachydermous swimming displays in the lake formed part of the entertainment available at the Pump Room.

Surrey Gardens had a spectacular glass centre piece containing cages for lions, tigers, giraffes and a rhinoceros (the Gardens were later to be rivalled by the Crystal Palace in this respect) and held huge set piece displays often including fireworks. In one week of August 1846 the following amusements were available in the Surrey Gardens: the eruption of Vesuvius, the Gothic bridge of statues, Promenade Concerts (featuring, *inter alia*, selections from Verdi and Rossini), Calypso's fairy grotto, the glass conservatory, descent of Phoebus in the chariot of the sun, the Chinese pagoda, the pyrotechnic display, the Neapolitan carnival (including the bands of the Royal Horse Guards and the Royal Artillery). All this came with plentiful use of gas lighting in "coloured bucket lamps". The Zoological Department, as it was described, was only one of the things on offer and in this week it featured a giraffe with a Nubian handler (described as a recent present from Her Majesty) and timed entry to see the feeding of the carnivores and pelicans. An extra shilling (5p) got you entry to privileged viewing platforms reserved "for the nobility and gentry" and as the nights with the Neapolitan Carnival had a two shilling rather than a one shilling entry it is clear that a night out at the Surrey gardens was not available to everyone.

As a zoo the gardens ran between 1832 and 1855 when most of the animals were sold off to Regent's Park. Although the gardens had been notion-ally motivated by the existence of a learned society they were much more explicitly about entertainment than the Zoological Society's more austere project. But they were not cheap to enter (one shilling) and nor did they lack powerful patrons (Queen Adelaide, the Duke of Devonshire and the Archbishop of Canterbury). Indeed, as late as 1850, one London guidebook suggested that in some ways the zoological collection at the Surrey gardens was better than that at Regent's Park. And you got more for your shilling. Queen Victoria plainly thought it was good value as she and her family visited in 1848 and she was described as the institution's patron.

A much smaller facility was the East London Menagerie and Aquarium which opened in 1875 and burned down on 4th June 1884. This included a waxworks and a museum and was, in some ways, a throwback to the earlier days of the indoor displays of exotic creatures represented by the Exeter 'Change. *The Penny Illustrated Paper and Illustrated Times* gave a full account of the fire and from it we learn several things about this otherwise obscure facility. It was housed in a collection of three large connected buildings with the menagerie on the first floor and the aquarium (with some of the menagerie animals) on the ground floor, loaded firearms were kept on the premises in case an urgent need arose to shoot an animal, the collection consisted of seals, ducks, a jackal, an elk, a wolf, a lioness with a cub, some monkeys, some civet cats and other smaller animals and various bears. Most of the animals did not escape the fire and many of those who survived but were injured were shot by Captain Burkett of the Honourable Artillery Company. The firemen did have some success though: they rescued three bears who lived together in a cage in the aquarium:

> The terrified bears had made their appearance at an iron-barred window looking out upon the thoroughfare running at the rear of the menagerie. The firemen had broken the glass, which lay in fragments upon the sill, and in close proximity to the bars, which alone prevented the egress of the animals confined within. Now and again the watchers without saw a black muzzle appear at the window; and soon were shocked to see one of the bears convey some of the broken glass to its mouth, under the delusion that it was its morning meal. The effect of this dreadful repast was quickly shown by the rush of blood from the animal's mouth and nostrils; but an adventurous bystander clambered up the wall, threw down the broken pieces from the window sill and so saved the bear from further pain. With the assistance of some

of the keepers, the handy firemen extricated the bears from their dangerous surroundings, properly secured, and accommodated them in a stable some distance off.

Alas, this was one of the few success stories of a terrible night. The Russian bear who was kept in the main menagerie upstairs, for example, was burned to death. In many ways, this small zoo with its attached museum sounds as if it offered many of the same pleasures as a visit to Jamrach's shop but without the added option of buying the animals.

Both the Regent's Park and the Walworth zoos needed stock. We have seen how this could often be provided by direct purchase from local dealers such as Cross and Jamrach or, further afield, from Hagenbeck. There were also early attempts at breeding programmes and these met with mixed success. Animals could also become available due to the breaking up of private menageries of various kinds. They could be donated by returning travellers such as Raffles. Sometimes London Zoo sent out its own expeditions. In 1864, for example the head keeper James Thompson went to India and came back the next year with a collection for which he had paid £1,516 and which included two rhinos and a number of rare birds. Some of these birds were donated by a rich Indian, Rajendro Mullick Baradur, who had his own private zoo at Calcutta and he added to a collection which had been subsidised by gifts of £100 each from Queen Victoria, the Marquess of Breadalbane and Lord Hill. This shows the levels and kind of support that the zoo could draw on and this support (both qualitative and quantitative) placed it in an entirely different league from competing institutions such as the Surrey Gardens. Clarence Bartlett was funded to go to Surinam to procure a manatee which he did but, alas, the creature died on the voyage home. Alexander Lecompte, a sea-lion specialist, was given £500 to go to the Falkland Islands to collect as many sea-lions as he could. He found that far from being the common sight they used to be they had now become rare and managed to find only four young animals all but one of which died on the voyage home from Montevideo. There were also individual donations such a giant tortoise from Lord Walter Rothschild and a water buffalo which had been touring England with a Rajah who preferred buffalo to cow's milk. He sent it to the zoo by post and it arrived in a parcel van with its head sticking out the back. In 1876 the Prince of Wales donated his Indian collection of five tigers, seven leopards, two bears and four elephants as well as numerous birds and small deer all of which had to be fetched from India via the Suez Canal. None of these animals died *en route* and although the opening of the canal did much to damage the British animal trade it also did much to improve mortality rates of transported creatures who now had a far less arduous voyage before them.

Finally, all manner of individuals gave animals to the zoo. Many of these, especially it appears those given by ladies, were monkeys which had once been pets but had become too difficult to manage or had bitten someone. The traveller Arthur Adams bought two bears and two giant salamanders and a collection of smaller animals during a visit to Japan and presented them to the zoo in 1859. Sometimes the dealers themselves gave unsellable animals away – such as a twenty-two foot long anaconda that came from Edward Cross. Australian animals were a strong feature of the zoo and a colony of free-flying crested pigeons were acclimatised within the gardens. There were also kangaroos, Tasmanian Devils, dasyures, wombats (as we have seen) and the now extinct Tasmanian tiger. In 1881 the zoo opened the world's first ever insect house (the Insectorium) and people could see exotic butterflies and moths as well as a large exhibition of silk worms. The Insect House had its own guidebook featuring the massive Indian Moon Moth on the cover.

The zoo had various famous animals which created small cults of their own. In 1836 King William IV gave a pair of giraffes which started a breeding line that continued unbroken for fifty years and spurred a bout of *giraffomania* mirroring the fashion that had been sparked by the giraffe Zarafa in France. These did better than the first giraffe to be seen in England which arrived in 1827 and was dead by 1829 – this was due to George IV taking an interest in her and deciding that a diet consisting only of milk was what a giraffe must need. In the last year of her life what can only be described as a Zimmer frame was made for her as her royally decreed diet had made her so weak she could barely stand.

By 1847 the worrying financial position of the zoo led the Zoological Society's new Secretary D. W. Mitchell (who subsequently took up the post of Superintendent at the *Jardin d'Acclimatation* in Paris) not only to liberalise the entry regime but also to embark on a new campaign of designating "star" animals in order to raise funds without going down market by putting on firework displays, although he did institute concerts on Saturday afternoons. These animals would be specially displayed and advertised and, in some cases, decisions to acquire specific creatures were made with the specific intention of creating a new star. Obaysch the hippopotamus was the first of these and lived in the zoo from 1850 to 1878. He arrived as a baby having been captured on the Nile by a hunting party sent out by Abbas Pasha the Viceroy of Egypt and subsequently presented to the Zoological Society. Obaysch grew to be a great favourite. Queen Victoria visited him several times, Charles Dickens wrote about him *Household Words* and he had a comic obituary in *Punch* and a more serious one in *The Times*. Obaysch spawned a minor craze of *hippomania* and you could buy little silver models of him. There was even a dance called the *Hippopotamus Quadrille*. Obaysch had a special bath and watching him swim in it was part of the star process. His full-time African keeper, Hamet, wore native dress and had two assistants who gave snake-charming displays. It would appear that in the first year of Obaysch's life at the zoo the number of visitors went up by 191,000. Some of these would be accounted for by the new pricing structure but perhaps the majority was there to see a hippopotamus.

Other celebrity inmates of the zoo's early days included Jane who was the first orangutan to be seen in England. She arrived in 1837 and there is a picture of her nattily dressed in what looks like a Fair Isle pullover and short trousers. Her successor Jenny arrived in 1842 and she wore similar clothes as well as enjoying a cup of tea. She sometimes wore a hat but when Queen Victoria and Prince Albert visited, her keeper decided not to put it on her in case "it might be thought vulgar". Sally the chimpanzee lived in the zoo from 1883 to 1891 and was also a great favourite. Sally was an auto-didact and appears to have been able to count up to twenty, to use tools and to identify and fetch various objects simply by their names. In reporting her death *The Daily News* pointed out that she seemed to understand almost everything that was going on around her. In 1869 the zoo acquired the first ever live gorilla to be seen in Europe but this died after only seven months in captivity.

However, the popularity of all of these animals put together does not add up to that of Jumbo whose name is still meaningful for things of abnormally large size. Jumbo's story has been told in great detail many times elsewhere. In brief he arrived at the zoo in 1865 as part of an exchange deal with the *Jardin des Plantes*. At this point he was not unusually large for his age (he was four feet tall) but by 1881 he was nearly twelve feet tall and probably still had some growing to do. Jumbo was a key attraction of the zoo and rides on Jumbo formed a memorable part of the Victorian childhood. However, Jumbo was, unusually for an elephant in captivity, an African elephant and he was also a male. And male African elephants are not the most docile of animals especially when they reach sexual maturity and the periodic onset of *musth* makes them aggressive and more or less unmanageable. Jumbo went down this route and the situation got so serious that the zoo seriously contemplated having him shot. However, Phineas T. Barnum stepped in with a Jumbo-sized £2,000 cheque and so the elephant went to join the great circus in the United States. The zoo sold Jumbo against a background of public outrage and even questions in the House of Commons so much part of the English identity had Jumbo become.

The *Pall Mall Gazette* saw the zoo's action as the treacherous betrayal of a loyal friend:

> Is this the way we recompense our oldest friends, those best bene-factors who have given us the one boon which is without alloy – hearty and innocent enjoyment? After all the children he has so patiently carried, all the buns he has so quietly and graciously received, is he to be turned out at last to tramp the world homeless and unbefriended, the mere chattel of a wandering showman? What a reward for old and tried service! What a commentary on our pennyworths of insincere affection!

And so on. But the editors and journalists did not have to deal with a massive elephant blinded by lust and with only some flimsy iron bars between him and the soft bodies of his potentially litigious admirers. So off to the circus Jumbo went. But the adventure ended tragically. Jumbo was crossing the railway track at a halt in St Thomas Ontario on 15th September 1885 when he was hit by a train and killed – legend has it while pushing a smaller elephant called Tom Thumb to safety. He was stuffed and mounted but his remains were destroyed by a fire in the Tufts Museum in 1975. His ashes were collected and preserved and his tail survives intact.

Although these star animals were special attractions the general offering of zoos was not only a very wide variety of animals but the opportunity to see them in quiet and, generally, less distracting surroundings than the menageries. Even so from the earliest foundations they used the opportunity to interact with the animals as a selling point and a source of extra revenue. This could take the form of the buns sold for the bears, the extra ticket for the chimps tea party or the more substantial thrills of rides on camels, in the llama cart or, most daringly, on an elephant. These could obviously be perilous especially when you were dealing with a fully grown male African elephant like Jumbo. It is actually a wonder that people were not being killed all the time. Once, Jumbo was frightened by something and took off down the tunnel which linked the riding area in the Main Gardens with the elephant house in the Middle Gardens. There was plenty of clearance for an unencumbered Jumbo but none when he had his howdah on his back and he scored a groove in the roof of the tunnel that was still visible over a century later. Fortunately no one was aboard at the time but it was a close thing and henceforth a ride on Jumbo was not one of the diversions on offer. So although the zoos were ostensibly a more polite form of spectacular entertainment than the menageries or pleasure gardens they actually offered, at a price, a greater range of opportunities for very intimate contact with exotic animals. And a pretty good chance of being trampled, mauled or eaten.

Attractive though all these things were the zoos (Regent's Park and Surrey) had one big disadvantage: they were both in London so unless you travelled there you still had to rely on the traditional travelling menageries or local private arrangements to see exotic animals. However, this situation did not last for long as the example of Regent's Park was emulated in a number of locations around Britain and, indeed, elsewhere in the Empire. The civic advantage and the opportunity to be seen to be participating in the movement to improve public taste and, specifically, the behaviour of the working classes through the provision of zoological gardens proved irresistible to local councils and philanthropists and most cities of any note had at least one zoo by the end of the nineteenth century.

In 1831, for example, a zoo was founded in Dublin to be run very much along the lines of the establishment in Regent's Park and also designed by Decimus Burton. In fact, the founding collection of animals came from London including many from the Royal menageries at the Tower and Windsor Great Park (many more were acquired in succeeding years; the first giraffe didn't arrive until 1844) and the impulse to create an improving space in which the relationship between nature and empire could be safely contemplated was almost identical between the two establishments with an underpinning scientific and social rationale provided by the Royal Zoological Society of Ireland which had been founded in 1830. As in London, entry was at first kept at an exclusive level with occasional open days such as that declared to celebrate the coronation of Queen Victoria when 20,000 people poured

A RIDE ON RAMA AT DUBLIN ZOO IN THE 1880S

through the gates – which demonstrates not only the paucity of entertainments available to the working class but also the immense latent demand that zoos could potentially exploit if they lowered their prices. In 1840 Dublin Zoo opened its gates for a penny every Sunday and in the first year of the scheme – which was subsequently extended to include public holidays – 81,404 people took the opportunity to see the animals at this bargain price. As in London, the Dublin Zoo offered treats such as elephant rides.

The first rides were on Prince Tom – an ex-circus elephant and a great favourite whose skeleton can still be seen in the museum at Trinity College. Then Rama took over. This elephant died of pneumonia in 1890 and the corpse exploded catastrophically during the post mortem throwing the gathered veterinarians all round the room. An elephant *post mortem* examination is fraught with peril: in 1874 Frank Buckland did one for Jamrach – who feared that a rival had poisoned the creature – and on opening his kitchen door found that the removers had simply rolled the elephant down the steps into the area of his basement where it now reclined on its back with all four legs in the air blocking both entrance and egress. The removers, no doubt considering their job well done, were nowhere to be seen. Buckland

and Jamrach's man John managed to lug it into the kitchen where Buckland found it had died of natural causes – he kept the body by way of a fee and stuffed it. The next elephant was Sita (who was executed after killing her keeper) and, finally, the gentle Padmahati took up the role. As in London, animals were acquired in various ways including breeding programmes. The lions acquired in 1855, for example, produced offspring in 1857 and started what became known as the Irish Lion Industry. By 1876 ninety-two cubs had been born and this fecundity continued throughout the century. Some 215 cubs had been raised by 1901 and this made a very significant contribution to the zoo's always stretched finances. In 1872 the zoo received a shipment of sixty animals from Calcutta, courtesy of Lord Mayo. Dublin had only a small aquarium and reptile house but it was the first zoo in Europe to exhibit the extraordinary northern blindfish from Mammoth Cave in Kentucky. At the end of the nineteenth century Dublin Zoo had a powerful friend in Field Marshal Lord Roberts who used his influence to persuade officers serving all over the Empire to send in animals (they arrived in good numbers) and who, in 1900, took time out from winning the Boer War to inquire about the snow leopards he had organized to be sent from India.

It is not surprising that Dublin followed the London model so closely as this was really the only model for a civic zoo based on a private scientific society populated by subscribers all of whom were of reasonable wealth (Cross had also followed that model at Surrey even though his motivation was much more clearly and purely commercial). A rather different model was adopted by John Jennison founder of the Belle Vue Zoological and Amusement Gardens in Manchester but using the same pattern of mixed diversions as the Surrey Zoological Gardens. Belle Vue Gardens opened in June 1836 and although they were initially intended as a genteel and improving entertainment they did not require the reality or fiction of a learned society to give them a *raison d'être* as the intention was always to create a commercial entity with a zoo at its centre. Jennison had always seen the commercial advantages of animal displays and had started his career as a zookeeper in 1828 by building an aviary and monkey house at the back of his pub in Stockport. By 1836 Jennison had bought the Belle Vue site and the aviary now formed part of a complex of lakes, gardens, mazes and a growing collection of animals including lions and elephants and, eventually, breeding populations of jaguars and tigers. Belle Vue was very much a family business and we learn from a piece in *The Bradford Observer* of 15th December 1859 that Jennison and his four sons kept everything in their own hands:

They rear their own beasts for the tables of the guests and carnivorii. They milk their own cows – grow all the vegetables, watercress, fruit used on the establishment.

They are their own architects – make their own bricks [in fact, the near million bricks used to build the perimeter wall were baked in Jennison's brick works using the clay left over from the excavation of the large boating lakes] – print their own bills. In a printing establishment on the premises, 20 men now at work under the superintendence of one of the young masters, evidently *au fait* in all belonging to the craft. All those huge posters and small handbills, relative to the garden, rails, or 'buses running to it are issues thence.

They carve their own statuary – make their own fireworks – manufacture their own gas – make and bake their own bread, pies and pastry, including the famed Eccles cake, in perfection. They churn their own butter – brew their own beer – import the toys for their bazaar – are their own landscape gardeners. They run their own omnibuses and horses to and fro the gardens [one service was a station pick-up for first class rail passengers who wished to visit the zoo] – and have their own special trains for miles around.

This was enterprise on a grand scale and it paid well. By 1859 the improving atmosphere was such that "a drunken person was a rarer specimen than many of the caged animals". I doubt that we should imagine that an attraction like Belle Vue was available to that section of the working class that Engels – who was in Manchester working in his father's cotton mill at the time – would have described as the proletariat, as it would have been too expensive. But it plainly appealed to that very large section of the poorer population who had a little discretionary income and were motivated to spend it on educational leisure.

Belle Vue was, at first aimed at an upscale visitor. Entrance was by subscription only at ten shillings (50p) for a family and five shillings (25p) for an individual. To gain entry to the gardens you had to be respectably dressed and the last bus left at 6.00 pm which made it too late for working class visitors to make their way out from the city after work. This policy was

not profitable and by 1842 Jennison had dropped the price to four pence (1.5p) for a day ticket and was exploiting the fact that the railway passed beside the gardens and gave ready access to a bigger crowd. By 1848 class struggle was in full cry on the dance floors and working-class men were embarrassing better-off ladies by inviting them to the gavotte. This was better than the Chartists or Communists I suppose and it did not deter Jennison who continued to build his empire and added many more attractions to the Belle Vue site as well as buying significant parcels of adjacent land. But the reason people went there was to see the animals. The monkey house (built in 1881 as a palace in the Moorish style) offered much entertainment both for the visitors and the monkeys as the latter had a water pump, a machine that enabled them to draw up their own food and grind their own corn, rocking horses and fixed wheels, like hamster wheels, for them to exercise themselves and, of course, work to earn their keep in a most suitably Victorian manner. Conversely, another Belle Vue entertainment was rabbit coursing which is a less attractive form of engagement with animals.

The guide book for 1892 gives a wonderful flavour of Belle Vue at the height of its attractiveness and shows very clearly that the secret of its commercial success was due not only to the mixture of its entertainments but also to the shrewd blend of commercial opportunity (once you have bought your entry ticket almost everything costs extra) and concern for the visitor experience (down to publishing train and tram time tables and fares from various parts of the region). Unlike other nineteenth-century zoo guidebooks the Belle Vue publication is heavily illustrated and has charming pictures both of the animals and of the various attractions of the park. There is a very long section on the current spectacular (a re-enaction in front of a massive panorama) details of the boating lakes, the mazes, the museum (with Maharajah the elephant's skeleton prominently displayed) the hothouses and conservatories, and the various refreshment rooms. A cinematograph was installed later. The main hall cost one shilling (5p) to enter but for that you got as much tea and bread and butter as you wanted with beef or ham for another sixpence (2.5p). You could also eat a more substantial meal and wash it down with some impressive wines: Bollinger at twelve shillings (60p) per bottle, and Pommery at fourteen shillings (70p). If you liked claret there was Chateau de Beychevelle (1870) at eight shillings and sixpence (42.5p). But if you preferred Burgundy there was Gevrey Chambertin at ten shillings (50p) and Romanée Conti (1870) at seven shillings and sixpence (37.5p). These must have been beyond most visitors' pockets so if you couldn't afford wine then Belle Vue's own beer was only two pence (slightly less than 1p) a glass. The guide book makes the animals seem almost incidental but they were there and watching: underneath the music hall, for example, lived bears, wolves, hyenas, pumas, jaguars and leopards. A strange combination of emus and marmots lived in an "eastern kiosque" beside one of the refreshment areas. There were three bear pits: one for polar bears, one for black bears and one for brown bears. The two Indian elephants gave rides and the sea lions dived through hoops and did other tricks. There is plenty of natural history to be gleaned from the guide book but even its entries on the animals concentrate more on anecdotes about them than on scientific description (like the guide books for Regent's Park). The animals were clearly the main attraction but Jennison knew that they could not bring back customers time and time again and offered a comprehensive day out to suit all pockets.

Much smaller menageries attached to fun fairs could be found at Margate in the "Garden of Eden", at Southend in the "Kursaal" (this opened in 1901 featuring a "Lady lion tamer" and, by the 1930s, it had grown into a full scale zoo managed by Bostock's) and although these were on a much smaller scale than Belle Vue they offered the same blend of exotic animals and a holiday atmosphere. A larger zoo was maintained as a breeding and training facility by Sanger's Circus on what became the site of the Dreamland amusement park in Margate and was a useful way of raising extra income

Chapter Five

from the animals when the circus was not touring. In Blackpool Tower, Dr Crocker's Aquarium, Aviary and Menagerie was an attraction between 1873 and 1893 when it was replaced by the less enticingly named Blackpool Tower Menagerie which kept going until 1974. A small menagerie opened in 1900 at the Tower in New Brighton on the Wirral.

When Wombwell's No.1 menagerie was closed down and auctioned off in Edinburgh in April 1877 Jennison paid ten guineas (£10.50) for a Nylghau (a rare Indian antelope). This was a bargain as the other one in the sale went for £26 to van Amburgh's agent. He bought a pregnant lioness for £105 and a baboon for £3 10s (£3.50). He also paid £680 for an eight-year-old, tusked Indian elephant called Maharajah. This was a big purchase as the other elephant in the sale, a small female, was bought by Jamrach's rival Rice for the bargain price of £145. And she could whistle and grind an organ. Maharajah became one of the celebrities of Belle Vue, not least because after he was acquired he then walked all the way from Edinburgh to Manchester. The journey took ten days and, not unnaturally, Maharajah and his keeper Lorenzo were a source of great fascination wherever they went. In 1875 a minor artist called Heywood Hardy exhibited a piece called *The Disputed Toll* at the Royal Academy this shows a man with an elephant arguing with the keeper of a tollgate and purportedly referred to an incident on Maharajah's progress south although there is no evidence that such a dispute ever took place. The more lurid story that Maharajah simply smashed through the toll gate was debunked by the *Manchester Guardian* which probably told the truth when it said that Maharajah had not been subject to any tolls as he was not on the list of animals who were liable to them. Maharajah was a great favourite at the zoo (where there were several other elephants) and gave rides until his death in 1882. His skeleton was mounted and displayed in the Belle Vue museum (another of Jennison's attractions) until 1941 when it was sold for £30 to the Manchester Museum.

Jennison's design of a commercially viable zoo was a novelty outside the metropolis and it was built partly on the failure of the more respectable Manchester Zoological Gardens. Indeed it was probably more than partly responsible for that facility's lack of success. Manchester Zoological Gardens was founded in 1838 and combined a well-designed and interesting garden with a significant collection of animals including kangaroos, marmosets, lions, leopards, tigers, baboons, polar bears, hyenas, civets, elephants, rhinoceri, dromedaries, wallabies, porcupines and dingoes as well as many exotic species of birds and smaller mammals. A keeper was poached from Edward Cross and stock was acquired from, among other places, Wombwell's menagerie. It presented a very different (and ultimately less attractive) experience to Belle Vue and offered gentle picturesque walks in place of firework displays and concerts in place of sporting competitions.

HEYWOOD HARDY *THE DISPUTED TOLL* © Manchester City Galleries

Chapter Five

The *Blackburn Standard* for 6th June 1838 gives us a flavour of the excitement that surrounded this new venture, at that point unique as a scientific fixed zoological garden outside of London. The band of the Royal Irish Dragoon Guards provided the entertainment and "we never saw a more dazzling company of beautiful and elegantly dressed women". A massive marquee designed by "Mr Benjamin Edington of London" was the scene of "*the déjeune à la forchette*" and if the arrangements for the human visitors gave cause for satisfaction the same could be said for the animal accommodation with favourable comment on the size of the elephant house, the general menagerie and the vulture aviary. The bears were sumptuously accommodated in a pit thirty-three feet in diameter containing four dens and a pole thirty-feet long, which had four branches for them to climb.

However, although the gardens were set up as a high-class scientific and educational facility they had the usual share of mishaps that plagued Victorian zoos. On 23rd December 1840 a young man called William Hardy was cleaning out the leopard enclosure. He had previously been careless and a leopardess had grabbed him. On that occasion he managed to escape but now did his job armed with two knives and two pieces of iron "thus favouring the presumption that he coveted a contest rather than the avoidance of one" as *The Standard* put it. One thing led to another and Harvey managed to let the leopardess out. She promptly savaged him removing most of his scalp. The uproar brought other keepers running and one set a brave terrier on the leopardess while another stabbed her with a pike. The dog caused her to release Harvey and then needed to be rescued itself by means of a blow to the leopardess's nose so severe that it bent an iron bar three-quarters of an inch in diameter. Mercifully the leopardess was then killed with a shot from a rifle. Harvey was taken to hospital near death and the terrier was, after a good shake down, none the worse for wear.

Although the premises were of high quality and housed an interesting variety of animals, the zoo was not a success and was closed in 1842. Some of the animals went south to Regent's Park, other walked across the city and joined the cast at the more attractive Belle Vue and some went back to Lord Derby who had donated them in the first place. In spite of attracting forty-2,000 visitors in its first six months the zoo could not survive, the reason being almost certainly the fact that the zoo had nothing to offer except an interesting and pleasant environment and a first-class collection of animals kept in state of the art facilities for scientific and educational purposes. There was a maze and some archery butts but these were calculated to appeal to a pretty exclusive class of visitor. This simply did not compete with Belle Vue and shows that although exotic animals might draw someone to a zoo it was the whole package of fairground rides and shows that kept them coming back.

An echo of the old Victorian pleasure gardens can still be heard and enjoyed in the Botanic Gardens at Churchtown, a suburb of Southport in the north-west of England. This was founded as a commercial venture by the Southport and Churchtown Botanical Gardens and Museum Company in 1875. Here one can still see ornamental gardens, hire a boat for a trip down an artificial river, watch a game of bowls, visit a newly restored fernery, be educated at a small local museum, listen to a brass band concert, stroll through artistically created artificial grottoes, eat in a tea shop filled with the most wonderful inflatable toys and then marvel at exotic birds in a series of aviaries and a collection of guinea pigs and rare breed rabbits in some now rather dilapidated cages. A visit to these gardens still offers *in parvo* everything that a visit to the Belle Vue or Surrey Zoological Gardens offered. Southport did not have a zoo of its own until 1952 (it was closed down in 2004 and is now a paintball park that includes many of the old cages and enclosures) but local people did still see exotic creatures as the town hosted an aquarium between 1874 and 1900. This was in the massive Winter Gardens which included an opera house and a theatre as well as various halls and promenades. It also housed a small menagerie largely consisting of monkeys which you could see as you enjoyed a leisurely stroll away from the rain which is a year-round phenomenon on that part of the English coast. At much the same time the eccentric Melbourne businessman and philanthropist Edward Cole established a monkey menagerie in his famous Book Arcade which was one of the sights of the city.

But the people of Southport didn't have to go far for a more varied experience of wildlife as they could catch a train on one of what were then four railways (now only one survives) to nearby Liverpool where a zoo was founded in 1833 by the former travelling menagerie proprietor Thomas Atkins. That the enterprise was intended to be a high-class entertainment can be seen from the quality of the entry tickets that Atkins had made. These were large bronze discs with an elephant embossed on one side and on the other the legend "Liverpool Zoological Gardens. Established 1833. Thos. Atkins". The entry fee was not cheap at a guinea (£1.05) for an annual subscription. There were bears (including polar bears), all manner of water birds, elephants, lions, tigers, hyenas, camels, tapirs, deer, zebras, the now extinct quagga, and a very rare Javan rhinoceros. There were also ligers, crosses between lions and tigers, which Atkins had been producing from his menagerie since 1824. By 1837 the zoo was holding entertainments to rival anything at Surrey or Belle Vue and in this year the celebrated female balloonist Mrs Graham (who also appeared at Surrey) made an ascent watched by what *The Liverpool Mercury* tells us was a "highly respectable company". This anxiety over the status of the visitors (which seems an almost universal malaise of the Victorian zoo) was perhaps prophetic as although Atkins ruled his little Eden with a rod of iron and insisted on only the highest standards, a facility selling alcohol was established in 1857 after his death and the zoo also became an incorporated company in 1859. This combination of strong drink and the loss of a paternalistic hand attracted the wrong kind of people and the zoo developed such a reputation for rowdiness and disorder that it lost its core clientele and had to close in 1863. The animals presumably went mostly to William Cross.

Although Liverpool Zoo was a privately financed affair it was clearly very much seen as offering a north-western alternative to Regent's Park. The guidebook for 1839 is a pretty solemn affair and starts with the admonition that:

> Visitors are requested not to teaze the animals.

It then offers a detailed tour of the zoo with some scholarly notes on each animal (169 different species in all). The bear pit – where there were spectacled bears, American black bears and European brown bears – was a key attraction where visitors "may find amusement for hours". As at Regent's Park (which by 1834 had 274 species) the bear pit was clearly a place that you could interact with the animals. The 1834 guide book to that zoo also consists mainly of scholarly notes on the animals but when the bear pit is mentioned we learn that nearby is:

> A rustic seat, in which a person is permitted to attend during the hours of exhibition, for the sale of cakes, fruit, nuts and other articles which the visitors may be disposed to give to the different animals.

We have seen that in London the bear pit could be a scene of mayhem and it appears that in maintaining them the more scholarly zoos were paying a brief homage to their origins in the menageries. The elephants were the same and where London later had Jumbo, Liverpool already had Rajah who did give rides and Poodah who could ring a bell and pick up a sixpence – which would demonstrate the extraordinary sensitivity and precision of an elephant's trunk. The Liverpool Zoo guide also describes the huge panorama of Vesuvius that was a central attraction but its most valuable feature is that it tells us (as do the early guides to Regent's Park) where many of the animals came from. In Liverpool, as might be expected, many animals were the gifts of sea captains – one such gift was a rhinoceros which can only have been transported home with the intention of selling it or giving it to the zoo. Finally, we learn that there is a tea shop "conducted by Mrs Wynn of Everton." What the Liverpool guide book shows us is that the zoo was intended primarily as a place where people could learn about the animals and the book goes into more detail on their natural history than a purely casual visitor out for a good time might require.

In 1884 another establishment, the Liverpool Zoological Park and Gardens, was opened in the suburb of Walton, this did not thrive and was closed before 1897, but it did enjoy a royal visit by the Prince of Wales (later Edward VII) and had a famous chimpanzee called Pongo who alone was worth the price of an admission ticket. The ticket office still survives as a cafe on Rice Lane. Intriguingly the zoo's brochure stated that "All Living Specimens of Animals, Birds and Reptiles on Exhibition at Liverpool Zoological Gardens can be Purchased" and advised visitors to "Apply for Prices at the Office". I wonder therefore if this somewhat enigmatic and now largely lost facility was, in fact, a kind of overspill showroom for William Cross.

In 1899 the great philanthropist Lord Leverhulme purchased land at Rivington to develop as a public park which was subsequently donated to the people of Bolton. By 1902 this had, among other attractions various animal enclosures containing kangaroos, zebra, Llamas, various exotic deer, sheep and cattle, emus, peacocks, black swans and flamingoes (one of which can still be seen in the taxidermy section of Bolton Museum), This was a rare example of an open air zoo with public access. Unfortunately the zoo did not survive Lord Leverhulme's death and closed in 1925 but it was plainly popular in its time as much for the various interesting features of the gardens as for the animals.

The fate of the Manchester Zoological Gardens was not unlike that suffered by other zoos in the great and growing cities of the north of

England: Leeds (1840–1858), Preston (1840–1860), Hull (1840–1860) and York (1838–1844) all had zoos organised along the same lines as the archetype in Regent's Park. Surprisingly, Sheffield managed only a Botanical Garden which is still going strong and has at times included an aviary and an aquarium. Later Oldham (1896–1899) tried its luck as did Birmingham with two very short-lived zoos. One opened at Balsall Heath in 1873 and the other opened in 1879 on the site of what is now Aston Villa's football stadium. Neither lasted long. There was also a zoo and monkey house on what is now the site of Northampton Rugby Football club's ground for about thirty years starting in 1880. In contemporary accounts of the development and opening of the Leeds facility one can see the excitement and civic pride which was involved in the establishment of a zoo – and also the expense. By the time the Leeds Gardens opened on 10th July 1840 the Leeds Zoological and Botanical Society had already spent £11,000 on the lands, the planting and the buildings. The site, in the village of Headingley, had been chosen because it was almost always downwind from the belching chimneys of the industrial centre. This was a thing of some importance at this time: even on rural Coniston Water John Ruskin could often not see the lake from his house Brantwood (about 100 metres from the water's edge) for smoke and as late as 1902 the single test match played at Bramall Lane in Sheffield had to be suspended on several occasions while the smoke cleared. The reason that English gardeners are still so addicted to annuals is that their Victorian ancestors had to replant every year as everything was choked and stunted by the pollution. The opening ceremony at Leeds was much the same as the Manchester event described above with the very same military band and the usual "large number of beautiful and elegantly dressed ladies". Although the zoo was funded by subscription there was a remarkably cheap (by comparison with other facilities) day ticket at sixpence (2.5p) for adults and only threepence (just over 1p) for children and servants. There was a constant battle about Sunday opening and some limited hours (which didn't clash with church services) were agreed but this didn't help the persistent struggle to make the facility pay its way. But there wasn't much to see: the zoological collection consisted of an eagle, two swans, various water birds, a raccoon, a fox, a few monkeys and some tortoises. By 1848 a showman Thomas Clapham had taken over the gardens and had a more extensive variety of entertainments and a cheaper entry to a renamed and relaunched Royal Gardens. But this new commercial approach did not save the day and the zoo was closed in 1858.

There was significant civic competition to open zoos and for very similar reasons. All of these cities had grown fast on the backs of massive industrial growth and all had growing working class populations which the well to do of the city eyed with a mixture of paternalistic pride and anxiety. What could be done to improve the lot of these people without paying them more? How would it be possible to address the main problem which was put, by Dr Williamson, the Mayor of Leeds, in the debate which led to the decision to build a zoo as follows:

> Every class of society seemed to him to require an object [i.e. a zoo] of that kind. The more affluent members of society required it as a affording the means of prosecuting studies most useful in their character and improving in their tendency. The operative classes especially required some additional and unexceptionable means of enjoyment, which to them at present were too much limited. It was a matter of complaint and just regret that the amount of time spent by the operative classes in situations in which neither their health nor their morals were likely to be improved, was so great.

And yet the zoo failed as did all of the other northern civic facilities. They were all set up with the highest intent, were of good quality and had special attractions such as Bucheet the hippo who lived briefly at Hull or the palm houses at Preston where you saw the animals displayed in tropical conditions. The problem for all of these well-meaning experiments was that they offered only an educational experience and when you'd had that once you didn't come back for a long time.

The same problem beset the early Scottish zoos (there was no zoo in Wales until 1900 when one was set up in Cardiff). Edinburgh lasted from 1839–1865 in spite of having a full-size blue whale skeleton as its draw card. Oddly it seems to have been the inclusion of fairground attractions that killed off this worthy civic facility and I suspect it went the same way as Liverpool Zoo once strong drink was made available. Glasgow had various exotic animal facilities in the Victorian period. The first and biggest was the Glasgow Zoological Gardens which opened in and was very much based, it appears, on the example set by Liverpool and, in fact, it was organised by Thomas Atkins – he had done shows in Glasgow before exhibiting a rhinoceros over Christmas 1835. The zoo opened in 1840 and seems to have closed by 1843 never having contained many animals beyond an eagle, a goat and an ape.

But there were also alpacas and it is possible that the zoo was founded as part of an acclimatisation venture. More notable than the animals were the firework displays and spectacles that were a nightly event. But these were plainly not enough to keep the business solvent and I suspect it folded as soon as Atkins absented himself from direct management.

The Scottish Zoo and Variety Circus opened in 1897 and was an offshoot of Bostock's menagerie business. One of its chief attractions was a large elephant called Sir Roger who had once pulled one of Bostock's wagons. He developed *musth* in 1900 and had to be shot and can still be seen stuffed (together with a smaller elephant called Kelvin who died at the Scottish Zoo also in 1900) in the museum at Kelvingrove. The zoo seems not to have survived the Great War. In the 1850s there were certainly monkeys and baboons on display in cages in the Glasgow Botanic Gardens. A zoo also operated in Groudle Glen at Onchan on the Isle of Man. This was set up in 1896 as part of a tourist attraction featuring a small railway and consisted only of sea lions and polar bears. The sea lions splashed about in a lake which had been formed by damming an inlet from the Irish Sea while the polar bears glumly watched them from cages on the cliffs above.

The bears went in 1914 but the sea lions carried on until 1939 when they were released back into the wild to take their chances with the u-boats.

A more successful enterprise was shaped further south at Rosherville just outside Gravesend in Kent. Here the Kent Zoological and Botanical Gardens was opened in 1839 and this kept going until 1900 with a brief renaissance in 1936 when the gardens were restored and a menagerie brought in for "Hospital Week". As well as the animals there was a maze and archery butts, a theatre, a bear pit, a gypsy tent, a café, and a banqueting hall. The Kent Gardens offered the right mix of education and entertainment which we have seen was a prerequisite for financial sustainability and also, probably, benefited by the proximity of Gravesend to London and the ready availability of a cheap rail or boat excursion which could include an enjoyable day spent at the zoo. But the entertainments available were very much of their time and when the business was auctioned in 1901 there were no bidders. This was also the fate of Eastham Zoo an impressive facility on the Wirral which operated in some form between 1846 and 1929. It had a selection of exotic animals including lions and tigers, a pretty fine bear pit (which is still there today), a band stand for concerts, a stage, some attractive gardens, fountains

THE SEA LIONS AT GROUDLE GLEN

and a water chute and roller coaster. Blondin himself performed there. By the 1930s though these were all slow entertainments and the gardens fell into rapid decline.

But most successful of all was Bristol Zoo which was founded as a civic enterprise at Clifton in 1835 and is still in existence as one of the most respected city-based zoos in the world. This zoo was the initiative of 220 local investors who subscribed the capital to buy, build and stock the zoo. Bristol seems to have managed to tread a middle path between the strait-laced educational mission of Leeds or Hull and the more festive approach of Jennison at Belle Vue. The zoo had a strong scientific impulse around breeding and the enhancement of animal keeping but it also hosted flower shows, held concerts and sports events and offered a boating lake. In this it was much more like Regent's Park where bird and dog shows were an important early feature and it even had its own character elephant, Zebi, who gave rides. The success of Bristol was probably based on three things: firstly it had a day ticket admissions policy from the earliest days and thus gained real popular support in the city; secondly, it blended its scientific and educational mission with other recreations sufficiently alluring to bring you back time and again but not so boisterous or vulgar that you might be put off; thirdly, its position in the south-west meant it was without a rival – if you wanted to see anything better you had a long journey and a lot of expense ahead of you and why bother with Jumbo when you could ride on dear old Zebi?

The craze for zoo building was matched to some extent by the craze for aquaria. The first was at Regent's Park (1853) with one being built at the Surrey Zoological Gardens later in the same year. We have seen that Southport acquired one in 1874. But many other towns (Brighton (1876), Manchester (1874), Blackpool (1875), Rothesay (1876), Yarmouth (1877), Scarborough (1877) and Tynemouth (1878)) also found themselves with these new attractions which added an extra thrill to the still relatively new activity of going to the seaside as well as, like zoos, giving a veneer of educational and cultural respectability to a harmless leisure activity. In the seaside towns stock would have been acquired largely from the by-catch of local fishing boats but rarer animals were also bought in, such as a beluga whale that went to Blackpool in 1877. In London an aquarium was set up at the Crystal Palace in 1871. This had massive tanks with a total frontage of 390 feet and with a huge variety of creatures including several thousand sea anemones each of which was fed individually with wooden tongs. A more

SEA LIONS AT OLD BRIGHTON AQUARIUM

spectacular show was to be seen at the Royal Aquarium and Winter Garden which opened in Westminster in 1876 with the intention of being a cultural institution in which study facilities, lectures and concerts would be supplemented by a collection of exotic fish. These included, among other things a short-lived white whale, beluga whales and manatees. But the establishment was not a great success and struggled on by turning itself into a circus run by "The Great Farini" (as such it is considered briefly in a previous chapter) which matched animal acts with such wonders as Zazel the human cannon ball, a marathon sixty-hour swim (in the tank once occupied by the poor white whale) by the famous Captain Webb and a general reputation for louche behavior. It struggled on till 1903 but did better than the Manchester aquarium which was converted to use as a school after only three years (it was massive but the need for sea water always made an inland facility a tricky and expensive proposition) or the Tynemouth aquarium which cost £82,500 to build in 1878 and was sold at auction for only £27,000 in 1880. There was also a small aquarium and aviary at Covent Garden.

The failure of the Tynemouth project, or the need for the Westminster Aquarium to rebrand itself in order to survive, shows that the aquaria faced very similar challenges to the zoos. Although it had a Winter Garden, a refreshment room and a skating rink which could also act as a swimming pool the chief attraction at Tynemouth was the fish and these were not enough to sustain the business. Yarmouth was the same and only lasted six years as the restaurants, billiards rooms, croquet lawns and skating rinks originally planned were never built due to lack of investment and, again, an aquarium that only offered fish was no more sustainable than a zoo that only offered animals. Only slightly more successful was Scarborough which after a very rocky start (it was built for £111,000 and sold only nine years later for £5,150) added a skating rink, swimming pool and theatre to the existing concert hall, fernery and restaurant so kept going, aided by the very favourable admission price of sixpence (2.5p) for the whole day, until 1914. Brighton did a bit better and is still going strong today. It had massive tanks (one was 110 feet by 40 feet) and a range of rare sea creatures as well as two giant alligators. It started with a concert hall, roller skating rink, rifle range, billiards room, café and gardens and was adjacent to the Palace Pier so it had, from the start, the right blend of animals and other diversions that offered commercial success to the zoos. A brown bear lived there for more than twenty years in an enclosure next to the restaurant.

Although it is out of the main scope of the present book it is interesting to note that the zoos in the main centres of Empire followed the same patterns as those in the home country. In India, they emerged from princely menageries but soon became places of public resort while, as we saw earlier, the East India Company had its own more scientific facility at the Barrrackpore menagerie in Calcutta. This lasted until 1876 and had a varied and interesting collection. Against this was the collection of Rajah Rajendro Mullick Baradur who started a zoo for his own amusement and for the entertainment and improvement of the public (he was also a significant sponsor of the London Zoological Society). Finally, in 1876 the Calcutta Zoological Gardens was founded at Alipore and this was a public project very much aimed at education and improvement along the lines of Regent's Park. Similar enterprises were started at Madras (1851), Trivandrum (1859), Trichur (1885), and Mumbai (1873). These were all public collections and alongside them were the princely collections which were also largely open to the public but remained in private hands. Jaipur, Udaipur, Baroda and Mysore are the chief examples of these and all had their foundation and heyday in the later nineteenth century. There were others too but the point is that in India as in England zoos were a focus of attention and the opportunity to visit exotic animals was seen as an improving and educational experience.

The situation was the same in Australia where four of the main seats of colonial government set up impressive zoos during our period. Melbourne was first in 1861 and was followed by Adelaide and Sydney (although animals and birds associated with the acclimatisation society had been displayed in the Botanic Gardens there for several years before) in 1883 and Perth in 1898. All four of these zoos were founded along the lines of Regent's Park and were initially the projects of local zoological societies and closely tied to the acclimatisation movement. The zoos did not therefore offer the kinds of diversions that were available at Belle Vue or Rosherville but they did almost from their foundation make sure that there were good facilities for refreshment (including providing hot water for picnic tea making) and in Sydney Mr Quong Tart ran a refreshment room and added a Chinese tea pavilion in 1885. They offered animal rides – at Melbourne on an elephant called Ranee known as "our Victorian Jumbo" – some concerts and spectacles such a feeding time in the lion enclosure. In 1882 and again in 1887 Melbourne Zoo included a native village where people could see the Aboriginal life that was already becoming remote from their experience.

We have seen that Australia was a most important source of animals for the English wild animal trade and although geographical distance made it expensive and difficult for the Australian zoos to acquire some of their stock (although some animals were cheaper than in Europe) the availability of highly desirable Australian wild animals meant that the zoos could do very profitable trades with their counterparts in Europe. Thylacines in particular gave them a valuable bargaining chip. In Melbourne the collection had grown to some 300 animals by the end of the nineteenth century and the zoo was specially noted for its marsupial and monotreme collection. The platypuses had a special enclosure but the zoo had trouble keeping them alive beyond six months in captivity. Echidnas did better but wombats, dasyures and Tasmanian Devils wouldn't breed. Only the kangaroos and possums formed self-sustaining captive populations. The zoo also had a good collection of rare primates and a large aviary which included Australian species. An aquarium featuring aquatic mammals as well as fish and an aviary opened in Melbourne in 1885 but was not part of the zoo and similar facilities soon followed in Sydney in the suburbs of Bondi and Coogee.

In Adelaide the origins of the zoo in the acclimatisation movement is clear from early minutes of the state society but gradually the idea of zoology took over from acclimatisation although the zoo's earliest collection was of native animals with some European and American birds and the loan of some llamas by Mr Phillip Levi. At this point the zoo also included an ethnographic museum. When the zoo officially opened in 1883 there were thirty-seven species of mammals none of any great rarity and things looked up 1884 when the former state governor, who had become Governor of Bombay, sent two lions and a shipment from Calcutta arrived as the exchange for some Australian animals that had previously been sent there. The zoo then continued to grow with the charming addition in 1885 of a series of guinea pig cottages for an innovative Children's Zoo. By 1893 the mammal collection was almost as extensive as the one at Regent's Park but although the bird collection was large the number of reptiles was significantly lower than the number in London.

One tradition that started in 1883 and has continued happily to the present day is the gifting of elephants to Sydney Zoo by the King of Thailand (then Siam). Thai elephants enjoy what must be one of the finest views in the world as their enclosure overlooks Sydney harbour and the birth or acquisition of new elephants from Thailand is a newsworthy event and explicitly part of the Thai diplomatic mission to Australia. A photograph of the old Sydney Zoo in Moore Park shows an elephant, apparently in an entirely unenclosed space, standing on a conical platform. A large seesaw and a cylinder nearby suggest that it did other tricks too and certainly a small crowd has gathered to watch. A small camel is wandering along a path in the foreground.

There were no zoos in New Zealand until one was founded at Wellington in 1906. In Canada a semi-private zoo was founded at Riverdale just outside Toronto in 1888 and struggled on until 1974 when the modern Metropolitan Toronto Zoo was opened. There were also modest municipal menageries at Winnipeg and Vancouver and at Sault-Montmorency near Quebec a small collection was exhibited by two fur traders.

As this survey of nineteenth-century British zoos shows, there were very many opportunities to see exotic animals without necessarily travelling very far if you lived in the industrial conurbation of the north, the south east or the hinterland of Bristol (then much more important as a town than it is now). These were organised along various lines but it is clear that from the point of view of commercial viability and, hence, institutional longevity the facilities founded by individual entrepreneurs which offered a massive range of entertainments alongside the animal display were the more attractive. Animals were good for getting people to the zoo but they would not be enough to keep them coming back. So for zoo visitors the experience of seeing exotic creatures was largely one that took its place alongside the fun of a fairground ride, the thrills of an elaborate firework display, the novelty of a balloonist and the pleasures of an overpriced tea and cake. However, this experience was, as we have seen, a long way from the more robust pleasures of the travelling or fixed menagerie. The audiences for both must have overlapped considerably (as did the management and handling personnel) but we can see, consistently, in the accounts and descriptions of these early zoos how anxiety about class drove the specific architecture of their experience and how they functioned as engines of social advancement where the families of aspirational workers bent on self-improvement through delayed gratification enjoyed themselves as they confronted tigers, bears and hippos.

CHAPTER SIX

The Private Menageries -
Exit Pursued by a Bear

It was bad enough to be kept as a prisoner of war away from your loved ones and la patrie but better to be in an English milord's country house than in one of the dreadful hulks off Portsmouth where food was in short supply and fearful fevers and diseases swept through the population like charges of grapeshot. The common soldiers there could buy some extra food with scrimshaw work but not breathing the fresh air and never feeling the steadiness of the land underneath your feet must be hell. No. it was better to be in a town and to walk the three miles on a Sunday to attend mass in the devout milord's private chapel and then to have a chance to wander in the grounds before making the slow journey back into the open prison of Chesterfield. It was actually a slightly longer distance but the gentil milord had had the milestone moved away from his gates so that the officers could visit him without breaking their parole to go no more than three miles out of town.

These are the thoughts that were going through Capitaine Pierre Duchêne's mind as he took a constitutional around the gardens of Sir Thomas Windsor Hunloke's Wingerworth Hall in the late spring of 1809. He hoped that he would be going home soon to his wife and young daughter and that the fortunes of war were still with the Emperor and that the year since that day in Spain when two English light dragoons cornered him and he handed over his sword (the Colonel of the Light Dragoons kindly returned it later) would not turn into another two or three.

Suddenly Duchêne's world changed forever. As he strolled and daydreamed of his return to France he started down a broad allée fringed with thick rhododendron bushes and overhung by pleached lime trees, their branches meeting across the walk like the swords of the officers who had formed the guard of honour at his wedding. There was a rustle and a scuffle in one of the rhododendrons and a shower of crimson-pink petals fell to the grass reminding Duchêne uneasily of slivers of flesh. A huge black shape began to emerge. At first Duchêne thought it must be a dog and he was aware that Sir Thomas, like many English gentlemen, was fond of his hounds and allowed them, as no Frenchman would ever do, to wander at liberty in his private apartments and even sleep on his bed. But this was bigger than any dog the Capitaine had seen and he watched stock still as it emerged from the bush and then reared up on its thick hind legs and reared and reared until it was over six feet tall and towered above him. It was a black bear and a big one. Duchêne took to his heels and kept running until he reached Chesterfield. Whether the bear had followed him he didn't know as in all that long three miles he never looked back.

Duchêne finally went home in 1814 but he never again stirred from his apartments in Chesterfield and had to be accompanied all the way, in a carriage with closed blinds, to the ship that would take him back across La Manche.

The menagerie at Wingerworth was, in 1809, still a very informal affair. Sir Thomas kept most of his animals in the stable and, by the time of the fictitious Duchêne's encounter with the bear (Duchêne is fictitious but the incident and its main details are not) the collection was getting so big that Sir Thomas had moved some of the animals into the hall with him. What these were is not recorded but at this time he had monkeys, bears, wolves and exotic birds. So there must have been some interesting encounters in the corridors of Wingerworth as well as in the gardens. Perhaps because of the bear incident Sir Thomas commissioned the great landscape architect Sir Humphrey Repton to redesign the grounds and to include a purpose-built house for the menagerie. The aim was to provide a new landscape in which the animals would display to their best advantage and, in addition, there was to be a rustic cottage with a room with three windows offering Lady

Hunloke the chance to view the creatures as they wandered around their new enclosures in comfort and safety.

In the event Repton's design was never realised and, after Sir Thomas's death in 1816, the menagerie struggled on until 1856 when it was auctioned off as part of the estate sale of Sir Thomas's grandson Henry. The sale was attended by more than 2,000 people and the animals attracted very competitive bidding. The animals sold were as follows:

Two Swedish wolves

A Swedish brown bear

A Russian black bear (very handsome)

Two American brown bears

Two Huskies (or *Esquimaux dogs* as they were called)

A Bloodhound

A Pomeranian

Two Cockatoos and a large collection of other kinds of parrots and exotic birds

The first lots (the bears, wolves and huskies) all went to Thomas Youdan of Sheffield who paid the impressive price of £88 and 18 shillings (£88.90) for the lot although this was, according to a contemporary report of the auction, significantly less than Sir Henry had paid for them. Youdan also bought some cockatoos and parrots (with their stands) and, for £5 10 shillings (£5.50) "Cantelo's Patent Incubator or egg-hatching machine" so he clearly hoped either that his new purchases would breed or he intended to go into the exotic bird fancy in a big way. Youdan was the proprietor of the Surrey and Alexandra music halls in Sheffield and so presumably he had in mind some form of animal entertainment or maybe a small menagerie attached to the theatre. Five people were killed in a gas explosion at the Surrey in 1858 and it was burned to the ground in 1865 and as the contemporary reports of these disasters make no mention of animals one assumes that they were housed elsewhere. He also sponsored the first ever football competition, the Youdan Cup, but that was not until 1867 so it is unlikely that he used the animals to add an extra attraction to that event. Sir Joseph Paxton was also at the auction and bought some emus, a macaw and an eagle owl to go in the Crystal Palace.

Sir Thomas Hunloke was by no means the only local squire or lord to maintain a private menagerie and his was, in fact, one of the smaller ones. As we have already seen, menagerie keeping was a perquisite of the wealthy and powerful (much like running football clubs is today) from ancient times and the royal houses of Europe maintained a wide range of styles and sizes of natural history collections. By the eighteenth century there were many more humble members of the English gentry who were adopting this expensive but showily eccentric fashion and private zoos sprung up all over the country. At Coombe Abbey, the Craven family maintained a menagerie based on the Versailles model with an octagonal pavilion. The idea was that you sat in the pavilion and could then see the menagerie which was disposed in cages all round you. A similar model was built for Samuel Russell Collett at "The Jungle" in Eagle near Lincoln. We have some idea of Collett's collection as it stood in 1826 when it included a range of deer, some kangaroos (always popular in Lincolnshire since the days of Sir Joseph Banks) and a family of buffalo. There were also exotic pheasants and what sound like coi carp. Sir Richard Hill inherited Hawkstone Park in 1784 and set about adding follies to the Gothic grounds that had been planned by his father (these included a tame hermit). Sir Richard's innovations included a troupe of monkeys who ran wild in the gardens pestering (no doubt) the herd of antelope and the black, white and golden fancy rabbits which skipped and hopped between the trees. There was a significant aviary of exotic birds at Osterley Park which were the subject of a *de luxe* volume of beautifully printed illustrations. In all there were by the beginning of the nineteenth century some forty-three menageries dotted around the country parks and gardens of England and these are just the ones we know about. Sometimes the word menagerie appears to have been used where there was only an aviary. We see this in a letter of Elizabeth Montague describing a visit to Bulstrode in June 1740 and her inspection of the macaws, pheasants and exotic birds in what was termed the menagerie.

We have already seen that one motivation for exotic animal keeping on country estates was acclimatisation but here we are dealing with exotic animal keeping for the fun and interest of it or for some reason obscurely connected to status or conspicuous consumption. Sometimes the activity could be very specific indeed. At Beauport in East Sussex for example, Charles Lamb (not the writer) maintained the Kingdom of Winnipeg. This would grow into a walled Gothic city with a castle, pyramid tombs for deceased "peeks" and two outlying towns, Faria and Lelia. The guinea pigs each had its own ancestry and heraldry and Lamb kept a meticulously detailed and beautifully illustrated chronicle of their doings couched as a chivalric romance. By the time Queen Victoria came to the throne the city was heaving with guinea pigs the offspring of the original King Geeny and Queen Cavia and an army of "raribuns" (rabbits) had also been formed. These were bad neighbours and occasionally broke into Cabbage Castle, as Winnipeg's citadel was called: "breaking dishes, spilling corn, eating all the cabbage, drinking or washing in the water, and bullying the inhabitants." This is a long way from the gentle Elizabeth Brightwen pondering on Jamrach and Fluff and we should remember that in 1823 when Lamb started his wild project guinea pigs were a good deal more exotic than they were in Brightwen's time. A similar tale might be told of Wotton House where the Evelyn family kept a menagerie of wild boar, kangaroos, exotic cattle, a zebra, tortoise, chameleons, a vulture and a seagull which were allowed to run, creep, lumber or fly wild around the grand terrapin temple where the family could sit in a summer house and observe the terrapins swimming in a pool below them.

A more significant collection of animals kept by someone of higher social standing than Lamb was the menagerie maintained at Horton in Northamptonshire by Lord Halifax. This was kept in an ornate building decorated with painted plaster urns representing the animals of four continents and a fashionable shell grotto. The building contained six goldfish ponds and as well as various exotic birds, two tigers, raccoons, martens, an ermine and two "Havannah hogs". The building enabled Halifax to enjoy his animals in an exotic setting influenced by the twin vogues for the Gothic and the first wave of Orientalism. The fashion for blended architectural styles in animal houses can also be seen in the Gothic pagoda-like structure at Culzean Castle in Scotland. This overlooked the exotic aviary and was built for the Marquess of Ailsa's troupe of monkeys. The monkeys played in their modish accommodation while the Marquess and his family took tea in a purpose-built dining room on the top floor. From this room they could also contemplate their ducks who lived on an island in a Gothic duck-house. Lord Halifax's neighbour, the Earl of Northampton, kept a menagerie at his house at Castle Ashby. This consisted mainly of exotic birds but there were also animals including a mongoose. At Eaton Hall the Duke of Westminster had Alfred Waterhouse build him a parrot house with a hypocaust heating system to create a jungly atmosphere in which his birds would feel at home and thrive. This was completed in 1883 and replaced a conservatory in which, I suspect, exotic birds had also been kept.

THE MONKEY PAGODA AT CULZEAN CASTLE

At Wentworth Woodhouse in Yorkshire the Earl Fitzwilliam was a serious zoologist and not only collected a significant menagerie but also kept meticulous scientific records noting how the animals were procured and how they were cared for. He was sufficiently concerned about this to use the services of John Thompson, the expert from the Earl of Derby's Knowsley menagerie. He had llamas, agoutis, lemurs, kangaroos, a tapir, chimpanzees and monkeys, an American bear who lived in an ornate bear pit with a salvaged stone door frame dating from the seventeenth century (the pit had been built in 1738, alas as a baiting arena, for a previous menagerie kept by the then estate owner Thomas Wentworth and consisting largely of exotic birds), a wombat, an emu, armadillos and various exotic deer and goats. In 1851 he spent £31 9s 1d (£31.45) on four llamas and shipped them from Chile at a further cost of £20 15s (£20.75) and as well as importing animals he bought them from other English collections. In 1850 one week's food for the private zoo included 56lbs of fish, 42lbs of grapes and "a bottle of port for the emu". He paid for dead lambs and sheep, for people to collect ants and gave a boy threepence (just over 1p) for a basket full of mice. The earl also kept a private zoological museum and many of the animals were preserved after death for display and further study. The Wentworth Woodhouse menagerie is one of the most interesting of the private collections not least because it was so meticulously documented and the records are still intact in the Sheffield city archives. In 1849 the Manchester Athenaeum Club organised a day trip there for members at Earl Fitzwilliam's invitation and the extensive guide to the house and gardens including the menagerie which was published for the benefit of participants is still extant but, unfortunately, it tells us more about the art on show than the animals.

A rather similar collection was maintained at Stubton on the Lincolnshire-Nottinghamshire border by Sir Robert Heron who was, for many years, MP for Peterborough. In 1850 he published *Notes*, a volume of memoirs in which he blended – with occasionally unintended humorous effect – his thoughts on the great public events of his life with observations of his colleagues in the House of Commons and comments on the antics of the animals in his menagerie. Heron was well connected and had two kangaroos from Lord Bath. Unfortunately the male succumbed to the cold on one brutal February night and he had to get another from Sir Joseph Banks who had plenty on his estate at nearby Revesby. Later he was in touch with the Earl of Derby asking for a male grey kangaroo as he only had "a disconsolate widow and one hopeless virgin" in his collection. He was later able to return the favour and sent the Earl a kangaroo and two "curassows" (cassowaries?) who had been raised by a hen although Heron admitted defeat when it came to getting turkeys to foster rheas. Edward Bennett's 1838 volume *The Zoological Gardens: A Hand-book for Visitors* records that the black swans in Regent's Park were donated by Sir Robert. As well as kangaroos and various birds Sir Robert kept and tried to breed from llamas, lemurs, armadillos, porcupines and chameleons. He also had a significant aquarium and was interested in goldfish.

Less ambitious was Henry Boyle who bought Eller How near Ambleside in the Lake District in 1863. He set about building a landscaped garden in the latest style including all manner of grottoes and ferneries. There were two connected ponds, the smaller of which was heated. In these ponds he kept alligators.

At Hazlemere Park, Robert Leadbetter was primarily interested in the breeding of large dogs, especially Great Danes and Old English Mastiffs. He had developed this obsession as a child when he had seen the Great Dane which used to live in the tigers' cage in Wombwell's menagerie. He also bred horses but the reason for his appearance in this book is that he had a sizeable private menagerie consisting of hyenas, jackals, Zebu cattle, a lion and lioness (the lion escaped at least twice and on one occasion is supposed to have confronted a travelling circus) and a monkey who used to attack any woman who spoke to its master. He also kept two bears but they fought and one killed the other. He had some sixty animals in all and by the early twentieth century was operating as a small-scale dealer with an exhibition at the Crystal Palace. However, the decline in the animal trade affected him badly and in 1910 he was declared bankrupt, having invested £7,000 (more than twenty-five per cent of his entire fortune) in exotic animals and another £7,000 in horses. Most of his animals were auctioned off to Glasgow Zoo. However, he was not discouraged and in 1918 he set up the "World Zoological Trading Company Ltd" to fund trapping expeditions on a concession of land in the Belgian Congo. The first foray netted sixty animals and earned Leadbetter £5,000 and the company managed to publish an illustrated catalogue and price list in 1919. However, it turned out that the Belgians had never actually granted the concession so the company was wound up and replaced by a new venture "The Arena and Stage Menagerie Company" designed to provide stock for wild animal acts but this too went bankrupt. By 1922 Leadbetter had only a few exotic goats and sheep, a buzzard and his dogs. Although he continued to describe himself as an animal importer there is little evidence that he carried out any real business and by the late 1930s he had sold Hazlemere Park and his other property and was living in a caravan surrounded by his dogs in which reduced – but let us hope happy – state he continued until his death in 1954.

At Woburn Abbey the Duke of Bedford had a menagerie building designed by Sir Humphrey Repton (which I suspect was rather similar to the one planned but not built at Wingerworth Hall). The menagerie was entered via a neo-classical portico and this opened onto an octagonal building which looked like a cottage and had windows on the front five sides and two wings. At the back the final three walls of the octagon overlooked a lake on which swam various ornamental waterfowl. On each side of the main menagerie building was a run of cages. The 1833 descriptive catalogue of the Woburn estate (*Hortus Woburnensis*) gives a detailed account, with plates, of the menagerie buildings and the plates show the water birds but we are not told anything about the creatures who lived in the rest of collection except for two antelopes who had died and were kept stuffed in a glass case in the recess of the portico and collection of canaries which nested in alcoves in the walls of the main building. The notorious German adventurer and amusing memorialist Prince Pückler Muskau visited the menagerie at Woburn in 1826 but his record of that occasion mentions only the birds and especially the parrots, ornamental pheasants and black swans. However, the menagerie at Woburn continued in some form or other throughout the nineteenth century with the 11th Duke in particular being a keen animal keeper. His efforts in maintaining a herd of Père David's deer at Woburn from the 1880s onwards almost certainly saved the species from extinction and by 1985 these animals were being reintroduced into their native China. Later in the nineteenth century there were lions and tigers at Woburn and after a lapse it is pleasing to note that the tradition of menagerie keeping at the Abbey was revived by the 13th Duke in 1970. The collection is still growing with a nod to its history in the form of a reproduction of Repton's original aviary.

Another menagerie kept by a senior member of the aristocracy was the 6th Duke of Devonshire's at Chiswick House. This included an elephant, kangaroos, llamas, elks, emus and a Brahmin bull. The four giraffes were one of the sights of London. The elephant Sadi was a great favourite too and was renowned for her intelligence. She died in 1828, just after meeting Sir Walter Scott who commented on "the dignity which largeness of size and freedom of movement give to this otherwise very ugly animal" and merited a short obituary in the *Literary Gazette*. Maybe Scott's less than flattering description sapped her will to live. The Duke's sister Harriet, Countess Granville, wrote of the "kangaroos, who if affronted will rip up anyone as soon as look at him, elks, emus and other sportive death-dealers plying about". In 1836 the Duke moved the bulk of the collection to the more rural surroundings of Chatsworth House which is within trumpeting distance of Wingerworth so the people of rural Derbyshire had a very good chance indeed of coming face to face with a surprising variety of animals. The Chatsworth menagerie was soon overshadowed by the remarkable conservatory designed by Paxton and rivalling the Crystal Palace (for which it was, arguably, a practice run) in both ambition and scope. This showcased the Duke's new interest – exotic flora – but there were also fish tanks with exotic fish.

The dispersal of the Chiswick menagerie just as the reign of Queen Victoria was getting started recalls the similar fate of the menagerie at Blenheim Palace's Park Farm that had been started by the 4th Duke of Marlborough in the middle of the eighteenth century. Interestingly there was a much older menagerie site in the local town of Woodstock where King Henry I had kept lions, leopards and camels before moving them to begin the Royal menagerie at the Tower of London. The Duke of Marlborough's menagerie included a leopard and a female Bengal tiger which was painted by Stubbs. There was also an exotic aviary in the grounds of the Palace itself. However, by the end of the eighteenth century the menagerie seems to have gone and been replaced by the kennels for the Duke's hounds. In the Victorian era a later Duke, the 7th, built an enclosure in which were kept a mob of kangaroos and a flock of emus but I think that this new venture was related to an experiment in acclimatisation rather than to any resurgence in the desire for exotic animal keeping on the Blenheim estate. Menageries which survived only as faint echoes by the beginning of our period included the ones at Petworth, Lowther Castle and Nostell Priory.

The menageries kept by the aristocracy and the landed gentry had their heyday in the later eighteenth century when the craze for estate improvement via decorative gardening and landscaping came together with the first stirrings of the trade in animals made possible by the new and growing Empire. By 1770 there were twelve animal or bird merchants operating in London and, by 1815, this had grown to seventeen if you include the fixed menageries which would also sell off spare or unwanted stock. In addition, the great families themselves had interests and friends that enabled them to acquire exotic creatures. For example the Bengal tiger at Blenheim Palace was a gift to the Duke of Marlborough from Lord Robert Clive – better known as Clive of India – who was also a menagerie keeper in his own right. In his garden at Earl's Court (then in the country) the pioneering surgeon and naturalist John Hunter kept zebra, Asiatic buffaloes and various kinds of exotic sheep and goats on the lawns while under a specially constructed mound were three dens where lions, leopards and other big cats were housed. However, by the early nineteenth century most of the menageries had been abandoned and this requires some explanation as the forces which were bringing more and more exotic creatures to England were, it seems, also shaping the ways in which they were displayed and the locations in which they could be encountered. Of course, one can never discount the simple change of fashion in which the elaborate pleasure grounds of the eighteenth century gave way to the more natural landscape gardens and the productive hunting, shooting and fishing estates of the nineteenth. There was less space for a menagerie in this new concept of land management and, in addition, ideas of aristocratic behavior were changing and the conspicuous wealth which a menagerie might so spectacularly display was beginning to be seen more as a responsibility than as a monstrous piece of good fortune.

Money was also an issue. Menageries were not cheap to maintain if you did it properly and given the cost of buying the animals there was no point in not looking after them (unless you were Rossetti, of course, who seemed entirely oblivious to the relationship between the care given to his animals, their lack of longevity and the poor value for money that this represented). We still have the butcher's bills for the Duke of Marlborough's tiger and these show that in 1763 she required twenty-four pounds of meat every two to three days at five shillings (25p) per delivery. So if we assume an average of two deliveries every five days that comes to £36 and 10 shillings per year (£36.50). In addition she was fed occasional calves' heads at fourpence each. If we assume she got one of these per week that comes to roughly seventeen shillings and four pence (87p). Then she had to have a keeper. At this time a journeyman could earn a pound a week but a domestic servant (who would have received significant in-kind benefits) might earn only two or three pounds per year. A really good groom might well be worth ten pounds a year or even more so let us assume that the tiger's keeper was paid along the lines of a groom. He would also have needed an assistant. A stable man might get only livery, bed and board but let us assume that the Duke was generous and paid two pounds a year for the assistant. Let us also assume that the in- kind benefits to the keeper and his assistant came to £45 and 10 shillings (£45.50) per year (nine pounds for clothing – a new suit for each of them each year – and a notional shilling (5p) a day for board). That gives a total cost for keeping the tiger (although admittedly the keeper and his assistant would probably have had other duties in the menagerie so their wages would have not been entirely attributable to the tiger) of roughly £95 19 shillings and fourpence (£95.97) or nearly four times the average annual wage of a labourer on the Duke's estate. And that doesn't include the costs of housing the tiger (fee to, say, Sir Humphrey Repton for design, plus ornamental metal work, other building materials and skilled and unskilled labour to erect the den), straw for the bedding (which would have come from the estate of course but still had to be mowed, dried and carted with attendant costs for labour and opportunity costs for other uses of the straw), veterinary fees and medicines – if a vet could be found who would tackle a tiger – and paying Stubbs to paint its portrait and then paying someone else to frame and hang the picture once it was done. And that's just for one tiger. One can see why Sir Henry Hunloke sold off his grandfather's collection.

The demise of the large private menageries also corresponds with the rise of the zoological garden movement and we have already seen how the local aristocracy often acted as patrons of the new municipal projects and how some zoos depended very heavily in the early days on gifts of animals from well-to-do patrons. Many animals moved from private menageries to public zoological gardens and clearly the growth in these facilities gave an eldest son or grandson who was saddled with an expensive collection of animals the opportunity to exercise philanthropic leadership and public generosity while reducing (considerably if he went in for tiger keeping) his own expenses. I don't suggest that this was necessarily a conscious ploy on the parts of the aristocrats who helped found the modern zoos but it must certainly have been an interesting fringe benefit. The growth of zoos also meant that the general public had more and different access to exotic animals and no longer needed to frequent the private menageries – which were often open to the public. For example, anyone could go to Knowsley to see the Earl of Derby's huge collection provided they were in a party of no more than six, applied in writing in advance and didn't show up on a Sunday. The houses themselves were open too (often at a fee – paying to see a stately home predates the National Trust or English Heritage). In the 1740s the substantial menagerie at Goodwood (which included a moose and big cats which prowled in purpose-built heated catacombs below the estate) was attracting between 400 and 500 visitors on some days. Not all of these visitors behaved themselves and one wonders if it was the experience of the private menagerie owners that caused the early zoos to be so picky about whom they let in. And so there gradually emerged fewer reasons to maintain a private collection. The aristocracy moved on and the state, in the form of municipal councils, or the market, in the form of zoological entrepreneurs like William Cross, Edward Cross, Gilbert Pidcock or John Jennison, took over the role of displaying exotic creatures for the admiration and edification of the people. At the same time the great travelling menageries started to achieve significant scale and, again, these supplanted the private collections. For example, if you lived at Woodstock you might have wandered onto the Blenheim Estate to see the tiger in the 1770s but by the 1840s you could make the easy journey to the St Giles Fair at Oxford and see a massive range of animals, some of which would perform tricks.

However, all of the private menageries discussed above look insignificant when compared with the two greatest of nineteenth-century Britain's private collections. These were Lord Derby's menagerie at Knowsley near Liverpool and Baron Walter Rothschild's collection at Tring in Hertfordshire. Between them these men built huge and important collections of animals and birds and because they were both conscientious and interested in natural history beyond the mere acquisition and display of their possessions they kept detailed records which enable us to form a pretty accurate picture both of the composition of their holdings and of the ways in which their menageries were managed. In the case of the Knowsley collection dispersal did eventually take place although Lord Derby's personal motivation as a zoologist kept it going long after most of his aristocratic peer group, and Baron Rothschild never did give up.

The Knowsley menagerie was the lifelong passion of the 13th Earl of Derby, Lord Edward Smith Stanley. He started his collection in 1806 when he bought a large collection of stuffed birds from a museum sale (there was in fact an aviary for exotic birds on the estate which had been built by the 12th Earl and which Lord Stanley the menagerist expanded prior to his inheritance of the full estate in 1830) and then began to buy live specimens of both birds and animals in increasing numbers and with increasing ambition. He also developed a natural history museum which was stocked not only from purchases but from the stuffed and mounted carcasses of the deceased animals from the menagerie. By 1834 the collection – which at this time was still mainly birds and exotic deer – occupied 170 acres of the estate and was costing £10,000 per year to run. The collection also included exotic fish and reptiles with the first ever lungfish imported to England swimming in a purpose-built warm tank in 1843 having hatched from the mud cocoons in which they had travelled from the Gambia. These came from the West African specialist collector Thomas Whitfield who together with Thomas Bridges (South America), Joseph Burke (South Africa – who undertook an heroic three-year expedition into the African interior between 1839 and 1842 returning with an immense collection for Knowsley and subsequently relocated to the USA where he continued to collect for Lord Derby in both California and Canada), John Bates and David Dyson (Honduras), Devereaux Fuller (India and Singapore), Louis Fraser (Tunisia) and John MacGillivray (Australia and Indonesia – whom Derby had used his influence to have appointed as naturalist on the survey of the Great Barrier Reef and the Torres Strait carried out by H.M.S. *Fly* from 1842 to 1846) formed a global network of contacts and agents that provided him with specimens throughout the life of the menagerie. He was also in touch with men like John Gould and Robert Audubon – who sent some Passenger pigeons which bred so successfully that they were released into the Lancashire countryside in large numbers but, unfortunately, failed to naturalise themselves.

In addition to importing his own animals Lord Stanley obtained specimens from other collections including the Royal Menagerie at Buckingham Palace (where Queen Victoria had established a small collection for her own pleasure and to keep her amused when she wasn't at Windsor watching her deer being slaughtered by errant pet jaguars – James I had kept a menagerie in the same spot before the palace was built) and London Zoo. Derby was President of the Zoological Society of London from 1831 to 1851 and the number of his acquisitions from the zoo was greatly exceeded by his donations both of surplus stock from his own collection and the many animals and birds he bought to donate to the Regent's Park facility. The Zoological Society also provided the first head keeper, John Thompson, and his assistant, Thomas Moore. Thompson travelled on behalf of the Earl to look at specimens. In 1839, for example, he was in Sweden buying reindeer. This reinforces the international reach that a collector with the immense resources of the Earl of Derby could command and in building the menagerie he did not hesitate – although he could be very sensitive to the price of individual animals if it was higher than he believed justified or usual – to expend vast sums. However, unlike an eighteenth-century landowner such as the 4th Duke of Marlborough, Lord Stanley was genuinely concerned to increase the sum of zoological knowledge in England and, in many ways, the Knowsley project should best be seen as an extraordinarily generous, if obsessive, attempt to create a facility that would parallel Regent's Park in the scope of its collection, the standards of its care and its scientific mission. For example, of the 605 specimens of birds in the Knowsley aviaries seventy-five were in breeding colonies. Thirty-eight species (in some accounts thirty-nine) of mammals were also successfully induced to breed. These were mainly deer and exotic cattle but there were also zebras and various marsupials although, surprisingly, the Earl only bred kangaroos – which did well in other English collections – with some difficulty. A particular success came with llamas, guanacos, vicuñas and alpacas. These South American species show the cross-over between zoological and scientific curiosity and acclimatisation for economic advantage very well as they are, in various degrees, bearers of high quality and valuable wool. In 1842 100 alpacas were shipped to Knowsley from Peru to set up a breeding colony. By 1843 these had produced offspring which were sold on to the Bradford textile entrepreneur and philanthropist Sir Titus Salt who had first started using alpaca wool in the late 1830s and was now looking to guarantee his own supplies by creating colonies of alpacas in the south Pennines. This was not a successful project in itself although Salt continued as the pre-eminent manufacturer of alpaca-based fabrics. Pleasingly, alpacas are now farmed in the north of England and alpaca products are commonly part of the cottage-industry craft scene in that region and people go on walking holidays accompanied by alpacas which carry their luggage in the hills above Saltaire, Salt's model village and mill.

Acclimatisation was also a motivation for some of the breeding experiments at Knowsley. There were particular experiments at crossing exotic cattle with domestic breeds for better meat and enhanced milk yields and similar trial with sheep to increase the quantity and quality of the fleeces. The Earl's first love in ornithology also gave him the chance to experiment in the interests of acclimatisation and he was a pioneer in, among other things, the captive breeding of rheas.

Because the Earl was so personally interested in the collection and its function he kept detailed notes as well as leaving a body of correspondence from which many details of the day to day running of the menagerie, the provenance of the different animals and the success or failure of various breeding programmes can be extracted. He also commissioned a *de luxe* book, the two volume *Gleanings from the Menagerie and Aviary at Knowsley Hall*. The first volume come out in 1846 and the second in 1850. This was edited by John Gray, the keeper of Zoology at the British Museum and was sumptuously illustrated by Joseph Wolf, Benjamin Waterhouse Hawkins (who made the full scale models of dinosaurs which were placed in the "Dinosaur Court" of the Crystal Palace in 1853 and which can still be seen, now restored, in the Crystal Palace grounds at Sydenham) and Edward Lear (who said his years at Knowsley were among the happiest of his life and certainly they would have contrasted favourably with the very difficult time he had when he was working for John Gould). The book was intended to provide more than a mere descriptive account of the collection: it was designed as a proper scientific study which would offer benchmark descriptions and illustrations of a wide range of species and so facilitate subsequent research. The Earl had several bound volumes containing his substantial collection of natural history drawings and sketches (including some by John Gould) and these too offered a resource to anyone who wished to research in the Knowsley Hall library.

The Earl died in 1851 and as his heir did not share his zoological interests the collection was sold off. At the auction it was clearly stated that the new Earl was not defying his father's wishes by selling off the collection but obeying them. The sale was carefully staged and there was some surprisingly modern viral marketing as the following note in *The Preston Guardian* for 6th September 1851 shows:

> The public have been prepared, by sundry unauthorized announcements, for the breaking up of the splendid and unparalleled collection of birds and mammalian possessed by the late Earl of Derby. The first rumour was, that the whole had been left to her majesty, but this was speedily contradicted; the fact being, that after the Queen and the Zoological Society shall have selected a lot each, [in the event the Queen chose five Himalayan monals and the Zoological Society five elands] the remainder and by far the greater portion will be sold to the highest bidder; if not by private contract, by public auction. In the neighbourhood of Liverpool, where the extent and completeness of the aviary is known, the greatest regret is manifested that such costly and beautiful specimens should be separated and scattered abroad; and it is yet hoped that some individual may be found with spirit and enterprise enough to purchase the whole collection, the vastness of which can only be appreciated when it is remembered that it covers 100 acres of land and 70 acres of water. The aviaries themselves, for there are in reality two, are perhaps the most picturesque and beautiful in the world. But our present purpose is not to describe. We may briefly state that, while the accommodation for the birds far exceeds that of the Crystal palace, the contents may be said to resemble the Great Exhibition in its variety and cosmopolitan character.

This was Great Exhibition year of course and the public was in the mood for big events. In fact, the Great Exhibition officially closed on the last main day of the Knowsley sale so that date marked the end of two major institutions. The Knowsley auction did not disappoint. The catalogue alone was a huge undertaking. It was prepared by the keepers Thompson and Moore and constitutes the only consolidated list of the collection. It cost five shillings and was the ticket by which one could visit the menagerie for the week prior to the sale. The sale itself commenced on October 6th and although it got off to a slow start with fewer buyers than was hoped, the heavy bidders from the zoos at Amsterdam, Antwerp (where there was already an annual exotic animal auction), and the *Jardin des Plantes* were out in force. There was Charles Jamrach and a representative of Wombwell's menagerie. Also there was Viscount Hill whose family had a menagerie at Hawkstone (see above) and who was now busily engaged in a massively expensive estate development programme which ultimately led to the bankruptcy of his heir. He was bidding heavily on Java deer and paid thirteen guineas (£13.65) for one male specimen, presumably to stock his newly improved parks.

Originally the plan was to walk the buyers round the lots and then auction them when everyone had had a chance to have a good look at everything but after a bit of this they obviously realised they'd be there all day and it was decided to sell each animal as they got to it on the tour. On the first day proper (the preceding Saturday had seen the sale of the specimens from the orchid house) most of the animals went to the European zoos with Jamrach picking up a female Molucca deer for seven guineas (£7.35). Day after day the sale went on, rather like a Test Match, with its own rhythms and reporting until some 315 mammals representative of 94 species and 1,272 birds from 318 species (not including poultry) were disposed of. On the second day the large and various collections of antelopes formed the main lots. Jamrach bought an antelope for £7 and the buyers from Wombwell spent 270 guineas (£283.50) on a pair of gnus which shows the rarity of those rather common animals in captivity at the time. On Wednesday it was mainly the exotic cattle – Brahmin bulls zebu etc. Thursday came the zebras, kangaroos, llamas and goats and other general quadrupeds. One male Burchell's zebra went to Atkins of Liverpool Zoo for £150. A quagga, which only had one eye, went for £50 while London Zoo bought a group of three kangaroos, one pregnant, for £105. Thursday was a notable day as the Queen was in Liverpool and actually paid a brief and entirely private visit to the auction. On Friday and Saturday came the birds and that completed the event with the exception of a few odds and ends which were largely sold to dealers on the next Monday, with Atkins of Liverpool Zoo snapping up some rare pigeons.

The Zoological Society bought forty-eight species of birds and thirteen species of mammals. Buyers had one month to remove their purchases and boxes and travelling cases could be had at the sale from John Thompson. A sense of the variety of the sale can be seen from the catalogue entries for kangaroos. In this category, which included kangaroos, wallabies, phalangers, bettongs and potoroos, there were some twenty-nine individuals for sale. These included a breeding pair of eastern grey kangaroos, the female noted as pregnant, which had been bred at Knowsley. Of the eight specimens of Bennett's wallaby seven were noted as having been bred at Knowsley. We know from the *Gleanings* that the collection had at one time had a Parry's wallaby too but that had obviously died before the auction. The significant collection of stuffed animals in the Knowsley museum was donated to Liverpool where they still form the kernel of that city's natural history collection.

It was expected that, as at many auctions, the sale would mean that many things went very cheaply. But, in fact, this was not the case and most contemporary reports speak of the good prices paid and the high average price across all the lots. The final sum raised was between six and £7,000 and this was thought to be a good outcome and one that pleased the new Earl. This was good as he had spent the Wednesday of the auction ill in bed getting up on Thursday only to meet the Queen. Of course, this did not represent anything like the price paid for the collection originally, and especially when you added the expense, for example, of mounting overseas expeditions. But it did mean that the Earl was no longer responsible for the estimated cost of maintaining the menagerie which was thought to be about £10,000 per year.

The Knowsley collection represents the point of transition between the aristocratic menageries of the eighteenth century and the new scientific and economic interests in zoological gardens and acclimatisation. The Earl of Derby was a pioneer in both yet the extremely personal nature of his interest and his hands-on management of the birds and animals marked him out as still belonging to the older tradition of aristocratic animal keeper. A very different story can be told when we turn the equally large collection kept somewhat later in the century by the second Lord Rothschild at Tring.

Before he set out on building his main collection (which is probably more important as a natural history museum than a menagerie) Rothschild had shown considerable form as a fancier of exotic animals. He had gone up to Cambridge in 1887 to study natural sciences – he was hopeless at classics – having already collected 5,000 birds, 38,000 butterflies and 3,000 other animals. Not bad for a twenty year old but not all of his animals and birds were dead. If you visited him at Magdalene you would have had to negotiate his flock of pet kiwis. He doesn't appear to have done much work at Cambridge and concentrated on his zoological interests to the detriment of his official studies. His money helped and even as an undergraduate he was personally financing specimen hunting expeditions to the South Pacific. He sent his agent Henry Palmer to Chatham Island to collect a specimen of every bird to be found there and then on to the Sandwich Islands where he stayed for three years making a massive collection to illustrate species variation from island to island the results of which Rothschild published in a three volume illustrated work *The Avifauna of Laysan*. Over his life time Rothschild published some 1,200 books and papers and identified 5,000 new species. His influence is perhaps best exemplified by the fact that in 1918 with the Great War still going on he had Chaim Weitzmann who had plenty on his mind negotiating the practical implications of the Balfour Declaration (as indeed did Rothschild) chasing round the Syrian desert looking for two ostriches which Rothschild had thought were in the safe keeping of one of his agents but had managed to get lost. The ostriches were finally located and arrived back in Tring in 1919.

Rothschild's motivation appears to have been entirely scientific and throughout his career he funded expeditions and carefully chose curators and assistants who were reliable scientists capable of forwarding his various zoological projects. However, he was not all serious scholarship and though he must have always had a whiff of formaldehyde about his person that would have worried most creatures that came into his vicinity he still had a touch for live animals. In 1894 he acquired some zebras which he promptly set about training to pull his carriage. After a struggle he managed it and by dint of including a pony in the key front nearside position of a four in hand was able to drive down the Mall and onto the forecourt of Buckingham Palace where Princess Alexandra emerged to give them a good pat.

The museum of specimens started in earnest in 1892 and was always accompanied by a live menagerie. But as early as 1888 he kept kangaroos (of various species including a black wallaroo which attacked a local child who was teasing him and was thenceforth kept in a pen – the wallaroo not the child; another escaped while being transported and bounded off down the platform at Euston station), a wolf (which Rothschild's groom Jeeves used to take on a lead down to the pub in the evenings), kiwis, rheas, emus, cassowaries, pangolins, dingoes, a capybara, a monkey, giant tortoises (on one of these Rothschild used to ride urging the creature forward with a lettuce dangling from a stick held above its nose; another, which was called Rotumah, was probably the largest in the world, 150 years old and was found by Roth-schild's agents wandering in the gardens of a lunatic asylum in Sydney; another one, a mere centenarian, was given to him by the former Queen of the Sandwich Islands), giant lizards which ate all the arum lilies in the gardens much to his parents' fury and various birds. These wandered fairly freely about the park and when a cassowary pursued Rothschild's father who was having a gentle ride through the park – being on a horse which is being chased by an infuriated cassowary must offer a thrill that few would wish to repeat – he was barred from buying any more live animals and could not continue until he inherited the estate in his right.

Rothschild's money makes discussion of the costs of his collection redundant. He would buy heavily in the taxidermist's shops of London and never asked the price of anything. Most people, once they got wind of the fact that he was interested in a specimen, inflated the price often to a ludicrous extent. He continued to fund his own expeditions including one to the Galapagos Islands and to maintain an extensive global network of agents and collectors. He leased the island of Aldabara in the Indian Ocean in order to preserve a colony of giant tortoises. By his death in 1937 his life-long obsession meant that he left a collection numbering 2.25 million butterflies and moths, 300,000 bird skins, 200,000 birds' eggs and 144 giant tortoises. This was zoology on an industrial scale. Like the Earl of Derby, Rothschild had a philanthropic motivation and left his collection to the nation – although the bulk of the huge collection of bird skins had been sold off to New York's American Museum of Natural History in 1931 when Rothschild was having financial worries partly caused by a long-running blackmail of which he was the victim. But even then he kept the live collection of emus, cassowaries and rheas which still numbered over 200 specimens. The museum is still a popular attraction although not all of Rothschild's detailed instructions for its care and preservation have been carried out and the collection of giant tortoises has been scattered. During Rothschild's life time the part of the museum open to the public included 200 complete mammals including a quagga and thirteen stuffed gorillas together with 200 heads and 300 pairs of antlers, 2,400 stuffed birds, 680 reptiles and 914 fish. Then there were the research rooms in which the rest of the massive collection resided together with a significant library of some 30,000 volumes. To give some idea of the scale of Rothschild's collection we can look at the British Museum's holding as it stood in 1890 under the direction of Richard Sharpe. This included some 230,000 specimens acquired by the strategic purchase of the collections of Darwin, Raffles, Gould and Hume (mainly acquired in India). By 1909 when Sharpe died he had doubled the collection again and the whole lot is now to be seen, amalgamated with the Rothschild collection, at Tring. But the point is that until the early twentieth century Rothschild's private museum was the most significant zoological facility in the country and represents the grandest example of the phenomenon of Victorian country-house science putting in the shade the small, but not untypical private museum at the Balfour family's Whittingham estate where Frank and Alice Balfour and their circle made significant amateur contributions to natural history and other sciences.

When we compare the establishment at Tring with the establishment at Knowsley we can see how the scale of Rothschild's collection was determined not solely by the desire for scientific knowledge. It was also shaped by the gathering forces of modernity. He argued that one reason for the sale of his birds to New York was his fear that another European war would be attended by the kind of indiscriminate bombing campaign that could destroy them forever. This turned out to be prescient as a large section of the Earl of Derby's collection was destroyed in 1941 when Liverpool museum was hit by German fire bombs. But pondering the vast numbers of creatures kept in various stages of preservation or simply as skins in the museum one is struck by a massive wave of melancholy. The cheerlessness which we encountered in the vast bird stock rooms of Jamrach's shop is somehow magnified when we are in the presence of nearly three million dead animals and if Knowsley represents the early stages of the nineteenth-century's optimistic drive for progress, Tring seems to exemplify its malign apotheosis.

CHAPTER SEVEN

Museums, Collections and Conclusions - In the Dead Zoo

It had been hot all day and now the heat was not only bearing down like a physical weight it was also radiating upwards from every stone, from every pebble. Even the sandy soil glistened in the heat and each grain shone like a lost tooth. The boom of the waves crashing in at King George Sound only two miles away seemed to mock the dryness of the desert and his cracked lips, burnt ears and peeling face cried out to be plunged into the cooling and astringent waters of the Pacific. At thirty he was still young enough to cope but it was not easy and the sweat stung in his eyes and caked hard at night in every fold of his clothing. He crept forward and beside him one of his two Aboriginal guides silently indicated a movement in a scrubby stump of spinifex. Beside the shrub two quokkas peered with naïve curiosity and no great alarm at the three men as they slid nearer and nearer. Suddenly one of the Aborigines lunged forward with his spear and all three men jumped up. Lying dead was a strange animal, its eyes were already dulled and a fly was already settled on the blood seeping from the spear wound and another on the bead of blood that had bubbled from its mouth. It was like a miniature kangaroo and also like a rat and was quite different from anything he had seen before. He would collect it and preserve it as best he could then carry it back to Mr Gould in Sydney.

The thirty-year-old in this story was John Gilbert who had been in Australia for two years working as a collector for John Gould. The animal was Gilbert's potoroo or *Hypsiprimnus gilbertii* or *Ngil-gyte* depending on who you were.

We don't know the names of Gilbert's Aboriginal guides. Gilbert was a skilled collector and on his return to England Gould sent him straight back to Australia where, in seventeen months he collected 432 birds, 318 mammals and an unknown number of reptiles and plants. Many of these specimens, like Gilbert's potoroo, were previously unknown to the European scientific establishment, many were already rare in that they were restricted to very limited ranges, and many would become extinct before the death of Queen Victoria. In 1844 Gilbert travelled north with the Leichardt expedition and on the night of 28th June 1845 he lay dead in the desert with a spear through his neck after an attack by local people on Ludwig Leichardt's camp.

Gilbert's story is an interesting one not least because the animal named for him is one of the most endangered in the world. It was thought to be extinct by 1909 but amazingly turned up again in 1994 (this is not an unusual tale for Australian mammals) and now lives in a highly protected nature reserve not very far from where Gilbert was the first European to see it or, at least, the first European to describe it for science.

The previous chapter ended with the dismal vision of the horde of stuffed and skinned animals in the Rothschild museum at Tring. This one starts with the death of an animal too and will concern itself with the final location where people could see exotic animals: the natural history museums and other collections. In considering these sites of encounter we will also meet, very briefly, a range of adventurers and men (largely) who travelled the empire and beyond to pluck all manner of animals from their homes, kill them and send them back for study and display in England. Sometimes, as in Gilbert's case, they didn't survive the dangers of their calling. Frederick Strange and Johnson Drummond both worked for Gould in Australia and met their ends at the hands of indigenous people in 1854 and 1845 respectively. John Carne Bidwill, who was mainly a collector of botanical specimens, finally died in 1853 nearly two years after spending eight days lost in the bush near Moreton Bay. He all but starved to death having hacked his way to safety through thick vegetation using only a pocket knife and he never recovered his health. He had survived collecting trips to Canada, New Zealand and Tahiti but the Australian bush killed him slowly. The American Perry Oviett Simons (not, as far as I know, related to the present writer) was killed – it appears for his clothes – by his guide, Esteven Paves, while he was walking through the Andes from Argentina to Valparaiso in December 1901. He was thirty-two years old. Simons mainly collected in Peru, Bolivia, northern Chile and north-west Argentina and a number of his specimens found their way to England as part of an exchange deal between the Liverpool Museum and the Museum of Science and Art in Dublin in 1900. It wasn't only the European collectors who met their deaths while in the field. Albert Meek, one of Rothschild's field agents, had a string of local hunters in New Guinea who shot the massive tropical butterflies there with four-pronged arrows. Meek claimed that two of his younger assistants were eaten by cannibals who sent him back the bones. This sounds to me like a whopper.

But although only some of the collectors died, the creatures they searched for almost all did. In earlier chapters we saw how dealers like Jamrach and Hagenbeck and collectors like the Earl of Derby mounted significant expeditions to acquire live specimens and how London Zoo would commission hunts for specific star animals. But live capture was very much the less common fate for most exotic animals. The majority that found their way to England were dead on departure. Collectors fanned out all over the world. John Whitehead specialized in the Philippines and spent two years there between 1894 and 1896 mainly catching rodents, seven species of which were new to European science. In Australia Gould had the brothers Charles and Stephen Coxen working for him as well as John MacGillivray who also collected for the Earl of Derby. Thomas Bridges collected in California and South America while Joseph Burke shot and trapped his way from Cape Town to the Magaliesberg Mountains from 1840 to 1842 and collected a vast number of animals both alive and dead. Alfred Russell Wallace was a specialist in two areas: the Amazon and the Malay Peninsula. While he was on his way back from South America in 1852 his ship caught fire and he sat forlornly in the lifeboat watching the parrots and monkeys he had collected beating a desperate retreat to the bowsprit where all but one parrot eventually died. The parrots must have sat there too confused to fly away or knowing that even if they did they had nowhere to fly to while the monkeys must have hung on in a desperate parody of a menagerie exhibition before dropping, one by one, into the sea. On his next trip, to the Malay Peninsula, Wallace acquired a pet orangutan in Borneo and tried to raise it like a baby. Unfortunately it died after a few months so the only orangutans that Wallace had with him when he got to Singapore in 1856 were dead: he had sixteen skulls, two skeletons and five skins. He also had 7,000 insect specimens and some 600 bird and mammal skins as well as reptiles and various shells. This was a valuable haul and it was sent back to England. Wallace then went on to the Aru Islands where he collected another 9,000 specimens, the sale of which enabled him to stay in the field for another five years returning to England only in 1862.

Amateur collectors who had the means could also be found in the field. For example, Thomas Wollaston was six feet seven inches tall and had a chronic lung disease which meant he had to winter in the Mediterranean and the warm Atlantic islands. He collected in Madeira, the Canaries, the Cape Verde Islands and as far afield as St Helena and was a friend of Darwin although hostile to evolutionary theory on religious grounds. The Reverend Octavius Pickard-Cambridge made one long tour to Palestine and Egypt in the early 1880s where he collected spiders. Also in the 1880s Edward Meyrick used his vacation time (he had moved from Cambridge to Australia and then New Zealand where he taught Classics) in exploring and collecting the insect life not only of the antipodean colonies but also the South Pacific Islands. Sometimes, hunting and natural history went together, as in the case of Sir Samuel Baker the Nile explorer and holder of the rank of Pasha in the Egyptian army. His pursuit of trophies in Africa, India, Ceylon, China, Japan and North America went alongside a serious scholarly interest in the natural history of those areas and the habits of the animals he shot. He also found time to buy a Hungarian slave (or rather elope with her when he was outbid at the auction by the Pasha of Vidin) who subsequently became Lady Florence Baker and travelled with him all over the world (except to court as Queen Victoria refused to receive her). She didn't like Baker much either especially after his equally celebrated brother Valentine (also a Pasha) did time for indecent assault of a young lady in a railway carriage. But, predictably enough, the Prince of Wales got on with them all like a house on fire.

Baker was by no means the first person to combine hunting with natural history. As early as 1838, the hunter William Cornwallis Harris was justifying his bag of over 400 large African animals by pointing out that among the slaughtered was a new species of antelope. In the 1880s and beyond, the intrepid Margaret Fountaine was travelling and collecting in Syria, Turkey and the Middle East, Africa, India, the Far East, the Americas and Australia (in other words the whole world). She had an adventurous time: she almost married her Syrian guide who was fifteen years her junior, when a band of Circassian brigands tried to rob her she peppered them with a volley of Turkish obscenities which so upset them that they beat a retreat and, in 1893, she was the guest of the Corsican bandit king Jacques Bellacoscia. Although she made many contributions to exotic entomology the details of her life became known only from her journals which were not opened (according to the terms of her will) until 1978 some thirty-eight years after she was found dying by a roadside in Trinidad at the age of seventy-eight. Nathaniel Rothschild (Lord Walter Rothschild's brother) had a butterfly farm of his own in Transylvania.

The great majority of the adventurous collectors were mainly concerned with plants, insects and birds. Capturing mammals either dead or alive is a much trickier proposition than capturing insects or birds and the use of the Wardian case from 1833 onwards meant that the majority of plant specimens (if they were being shipped live) reached their destination in good shape even after a lengthy and dry voyage. As we have seen from previous chapters this was never the case with animals. In addition, there were many ornithologists and entomologists and many museums which held ornithological, entomological and even herpetological collections but very few people or museums had the money or space for mammals and large animals. So the structure of the scientific establishment at the time also determined where the bulk of interest and activity was likely to be placed in the realm of field collection. In addition, the acclimatisation movement was just as vigorous, if not more vigorous, when it came to the economic possibilities opened up by the acclimatisation of plants.

Specimens came into the museums from all directions. In 1830 George Vachell, Chaplain of the English Factory at Canton sent the museum of the Cambridge Philosophical Society a consignment containing thirteen boxes of dried plants, seven paintings of lizards, two boxes of insects, ten bird skins, a dead bat, six edible bird's nests, eight lychees, two unusual shells and the head of a Mandarin who had had the misfortune to be decapitated. Much later in the century we find William Lucas Distant travelling in the Transvaal. He put together a large collection of birds and reptiles but only one mammal (a meerkat) and several human heads. His collection eventually went to the Natural History Museum. In Malaysia and the Philippines (he had previously been in Chile and Mexico) Hugh Cuming collected 130,000 plant specimens, 30,000 shells and a massive variety of animals, birds, insects and reptiles. His was a collection which, in the conchological branch, rivalled that of Lord Rothschild in that it was significantly better than anything housed in a national museum. Conchology is only tangentially related to this study as no one, as far as I know, was interested in collecting the creatures that inhabited the shells. But, as we have seen, it was closely related to the wild animal business and formed a significant line of income for the Jamrachs. In 1866 the Natural History Museum bought most of Cuming's shell collection and it was proudly carried in open display cases across the courtyard. This was in a high wind and all the identifying labels blew off and away into the London sky. There is still no final agreement as to the correct classification of all of Cuming's shells. Or so the story goes – it has been subject to several revisions over the years – and the truth may be much less entertaining if you are not a malacologist.

Collectors and acclimatisers could also get specimens, even of exotic animals, at home. The market places of Canton were full of animal stalls which had plenty to interest the amateur or professional naturalist, the acclimatiser or someone who was looking for a quirky pet. You could buy wildcats, oriental breeds of dog, birds and water fowl, monkeys, parrots and tortoises. It being China you could also buy insects and one of the more amazing sights that met the English traveller's eye would have been the stalls of the butterfly sellers. At first it must have looked as if someone was selling miniature kites but in fact the sellers had cunningly used ultra-thin cords to tether their butterflies to thin bamboo fillets and so they fluttered advertising them-selves more effectively than the stall holder could ever hope to do. You could buy these and you could trap and kill butterflies to send home but by the later nineteenth century there were at least four butterfly farms operating in England which provided collectors with specimens to kill and gardeners with flocks of picturesque creatures to enliven the summer days. Some of these were exotic butterflies so it is not entirely impossible that, while you leant on the wall of your cottage of an evening, perhaps smoking a pipe and happily contemplating your sole pig as it contentedly snuffled in its sty and crunched up the snails you had brought it for its tea, you would see sailing serenely past an animal that had its natural environment in the rain forests of Papua New Guinea.

The earliest and biggest of these farms was set at Scarborough by W. H. Head in about 1874 and by the early twentieth century (by which time he had moved to a bigger premises at nearby Burniston) he had a stock of some 400,000 insects representing nearly 400 different species of British and foreign butterflies and moths. Many of these went to be killed and pinned in the cabinets of amateur lepidopterists and also to natural history museums and institutes but some did go to provide living decoration in domestic landscapes. In Colchester, William Harwood had started farming butterflies in his garden at about the same time and although he concentrated on British specimens (which he also sold) there may also have been some exotic insects in his stock. In 1894 Leonard Newman set up a large butterfly farm at Bexley in Kent. Newman was largely concerned with producing British animals both for collectors and for people who wanted a good number of butterflies in their gardens (Winston Churchill was a customer in this latter group). Captain Edward Purefoy was not a commercial butterfly farmer but he does have a part in the story of exotic animals in England as he made it his life's work to breed the Large Copper butterfly. Although this had been native to England it had become extinct and so Purefoy's imported stock qualifies as a rare form of exotic and he takes his place among the early advocates of the now fashionable idea of re-wilding. Perhaps the most influential butterfly farmer was William Watkins who was also responsible for the foundation of the insectarium in Regents' Park. He had a farm in his garden in Eastbourne and kept and reared exotic butterflies sourced from his global network of collectors. He worked with Arthur Doncaster to set up the firm of Watkins and Doncaster in 1874 and by 1879 they had set up prestigious premises in the Strand selling British and foreign butterflies and all the equipment needed for serious collection and entomology (the firm still survives). By 1892, Watkins was an independent dealer and had a shop in Piccadilly where he advertised "British and foreign Lepidoptera in all stages". Interestingly, price lists from Watkins and Doncaster show that the prices of rare butterflies tended to decrease between 1879 and 1892 unlike as we have seen, the prices of other exotic animals and we must assume that this was because of a growth in supply met partly from the success of the exotic butterfly farms in England and the fact that transporting butterfly specimens, live or dead, did not pose the same logistic and financial problems as transporting larger animals and so were not subject to the pressures caused by the opening of the Suez Canal and rise of the German Empire in Africa.

Once specimens had been collected or farmed they had to go somewhere. As we have seen, this was the golden age of zoo building in England and many of the zoos also had natural history museums although these were usually abandoned once the zoo had taken of and eventually amalgamated with a local museum's collection. But the reign of Queen Victoria was also a golden age of museum building and it was to the new natural history museums which were built all over England (as well as elsewhere in the Empire) that many of the specimens went. In addition, of course, to the private museums which were attached both to the private menageries and to other large private collections.

As with the zoos, the new natural history museums could be private or municipal and while some were specialised in natural history other showed natural history collections alongside other displays. For example, the Booth Museum in Brighton started life in 1874 as a private concern open to the public and housing Edward Booth's private natural history collection. This passed to the municipal authority in 1890. Forerunners of this museum were notably the Sir Ashton Lever museum in Leicester Square and the "London Museum of Stuffed Animals" run by William Bullock in Piccadilly. In both of these you could see a wonderful variety of exotic animals but both were out of business and dispersed by 1819. The Liverpool Museum was founded in 1851 specifically to house the donation of the Earl of Derby's museum at Knowsley. The Horniman museum was founded in 1901 again as a private concern open to the public. Bristol had its museum by 1823 and York by 1830. Other towns such as Ipswich (1846), Manchester (1867), Newcastle (1884) and Norwich (1895), among many others, followed. Edinburgh got its museum in 1866 and Glasgow re-housed the substantial natural history section of its venerable Hunterian Museum in 1870. Oxford University set up its natural history museum in 1850. Many such museums were founded after the death of Queen Victoria but housed much earlier collections. For example, the Dorman Museum at Linthorpe was founded in 1904 to display a collection from the previous century. Others – such as the Manchester Museum and the Hancock Museum in Newcastle – represented the collected or amalgamated holdings of local Philosophical and Scientific clubs and societies as well as those donated by private collectors. We should also not forget Frank Buckland's bizarre "Economic Fish Museum" which went far beyond its acclimatising intention to display the exploitable wonders of the deep in the form of handmade plaster models made by Buckland in his kitchen to include all manner of other curiosities such as preserved boa constrictor.

In the Victorian period exotic animal specimens poured into local museums. In Kendal, for example, the museum was founded in 1796 and by 1901 it had a substantial collection of exotic animals on display. In later museums such as that in Tunbridge Wells you can still see displays of exotic animals all collected in the nineteenth century and now exhibited as much for what they tell us about Victorian science as for their intrinsic value as specimens.

The Natural History Museum at Saffron Walden which was opened in 1835 had a selection of colonial artefacts but its centre piece was a stuffed rhino. By 1845 the museum's catalogue shows that this had been joined by a stuffed elephant, a stuffed giraffe and numerous other specimens of taxidermied exotic animals. A photograph taken in about 1896 shows that these were all still going strong fifty years later and had been joined by a zebra, another giraffe and some antelopes. These animals were mainly donated by Saffron Walden residents who had lived in the various colonies but, interestingly, Wombwell's strong local connections meant that some of the animals were the dead of his menagerie.

Perhaps the best example of this phenomenon is the Natural History Museum of Ireland in Dublin. This was founded in 1856 as a home for the collections of the Royal Dublin Society and although the museum evolved during the nineteenth century it stopped dead, like my grandfather's clock, sometime around the turn of the twentieth century and now really has only one exhibit which is the museum itself. If anyone wants really to understand the late Victorian experience of an encounter with exotic animals pinned, mummified, stuffed, pickled, in rows, in glass cases, mounted in naturalistic displays, on the walls, on the floor, hanging from the ceiling, gently fading in the gentle glare of the gentle Irish sun or hidden, like precious watercolours or the illuminated pages of the Book of Kells just down the road in the library at Trinity College, under cloth covers which you can lift to see bright feathers and scales blazing as fresh as the day they fell into the collector's net, they only need to go to Dublin and they can see nature as it was meant to be seen in, say, 1870.

All of these museums had two functions. On the one hand, they were places designed to stimulate serious study and to provide the resources for scholars who could not otherwise encounter the exotic creatures in which they were interested. In this respect they were like the top ranked zoological gardens. Indeed, the frequent circumstances of their foundation in the collections of local scientific societies make them precisely analogous to the serious zoos. On the other hand, they were the descendants of the traditional Wünderkammer or Cabinet of Curiosities. In Tunbridge Wells you can still see a fossilised dinosaur footprint. In Dublin a jar contains the "longest tapeworm ever found in Ireland". These fantastic items alongside the serious natural history collections were what converted the museums from places of learning to places of entertainment or rather, to places where you could enjoy being educated. So they have a whiff of the menagerie or of zoos like Surrey or Belle Vue. But, as you wandered the foursquare displays (no interactivity then!) you might come face to face, in just thirty seconds, with an elephant, a Barbary lion, a warthog and a white-fanged mandril, its blue buttocks turned coyly to the wall. You stared at them through glass and they stared back at you through glass eyes. And then you went and got the omnibus home for your meat pie or your fried fish or your lamb chop with the kidney still in it, your glass of India Pale Ale or your Temperance wine or your Hocheimer Königin Victoria Berg Riesling Spätlese (they drank sweet and German in those days). And whether you were in a dense back street in Salford or a farmhouse on a Westmoreland fell side or a comfortable villa in a town less than an hour by train to London you sat by your fire, at the heart of Empire, with the memory of your encounter with the exotic still tingling and jangling like the sound of crickets on a hot Sunday afternoon in New South Wales.

Of course, the major museum was in London and this was the natural history collection of the British Museum. This was at first a part of the main museum but it was moved to its current location in Alfred Waterhouse's spectacular building in South Kensington in 1881. We saw previously how the Zoological Society agonised over access to the Regent's Park zoo and how various restrictions designed to keep out the working classes were a feature not only of London Zoo but also of some others. The same was the case for the British Museum and opening hours were kept between 10.00 a.m. and 4.00 p.m. on three weekdays only (until 1879 when it moved to six days and 1896 to every day) with no babies allowed and no lavatories for ladies. That pretty much ensured that no working class people could get in. This contrasted with the Hancock Museum in Newcastle which had evening opening sessions from as early as 1835. Other museums, such as those of the London Missionary Society and the East India Company, held occasional open days at times convenient for working people and were often overwhelmed by the numbers who poured in and were relieved that the horde did not destroy the collections, their passing marked only by a pile of skulls from the specimen cabinets. Once the museum was fully opened and especially after it had moved to South Kensington it was attracting more than 400,000 visitors per year most of whom would have been from the working class constituencies so feared by the early curators.

But while the early zoos worked hard on the preservation of their precious animals and even embarked on breeding programmes, the early museums were less successful at maintaining their holdings. The British Museum was worst of all and while it was first class when it came to bringing in specimens and attracting donations it was barely passing when it came to conservation. This was partly due to poor techniques, partly to inadequate staffing and partly to senior curators who might destroy specimens that they took against. For example, by 1833 the entire collection of 5,500 insects listed in the original museum catalogue of the late eighteenth century had simply fallen into dust while many of the larger specimens had been deliberately burned by the Keeper of Zoology Dr Leach who could not abide the sight of eighteenth-century taxidermy. But the turning point for the museum was the joint management of John Gray, the Keeper of Zoology and Richard Owen, the Superintendant of Natural History. Although these men did not have an easy relationship they were both serious and respected scholars who were able to stabilise the collections and make some inroads into the miserly funding granted by government. Between them they turned the Natural History collection into a respected institution and eventually a museum in its own right. The taxidermist Edward Gerrard worked for the museum at this time (in addition to running his own successful business) and took specimen preservation and presentation to new standards. In 1884 Owen's successor Sir William Flower divided the museum into a public display designed to entertain the visitors and a much more substantial research collection behind the scenes available only to the museum's own scientists and to other suitably qualified people. By doing this Flower not only invented the pattern for all subsequent natural history museums he also recognised the same dichotomy between entertainment and education that John Jennison had seen and exploited when he founded Belle Vue Zoo and which is, perhaps, best summed up by the circus proprietor Mr Sleary in Dickens's *Hard Times*: "People mutht be amuthed".

Just as the Regent's Park zoo had its more populist rival in the Surrey Gardens so the British Museum had some competition. In 1837, Sir Andrew Smith put on a massive show of stuffed animals and ethnographic artifacts at the Egyptian Hall in Piccadilly and this had the added attraction that the exhibits were, eventually, for sale (some were bought by the British Museum). In 1839 the Cosmorama Rooms staged a similar display of the spoils of the German explorer Robert Schomburgk's travels in Guiana. In 1850 an even bigger show appeared at the St George's Rooms. This consisted of the collection of the big game hunter Roualeyn George Gordon Cummings who had swapped the playing fields of Eton for the savannahs of East Africa and killed pretty much everything and anything that crossed his line of sight. Between 1843 and 1848 he shot eighteen lions, twenty-eight black rhinoceroses, thirty-nine white rhinoceroses, seventy-six hippopotamuses and 100 elephants. This doesn't include the smaller game such a leopards and various antelope and deer. All in all, the exhibition offered the edifying sight of thirty tons of stuffed animals including nearly half a ton of ivory. Cummings' London show went on until 1852 – and so added yet another supplementary attraction for visitors to the Crystal Palace – before it went on a tour which encompassed, among other places, Dublin and Fort Augustus. Eventually it was sold as a piece to Barnum in 1866. The Rowland Ward taxidermy company specialised in big game and mounted significant shows entitled "The Jungle" at the Colonial and Indian Exhibition in 1885–1886 and at the Empire of India Exhibition in 1895–1896. The Royal United Services Institution also had a good collection of stuffed animals and other preserved parts and was open to the general public at Christmas and Easter and on the anniversaries of Waterloo and Trafalgar. Like the dead zoo in Dublin this museum became, by accident, an exhibition in its own right before it closed in 1960. I remember visiting it myself with my father, probably in 1958 or 1959, and my clearest recollection – apart from the wonderful dioramas of model soldiers and especially the beautifully painted flat *Zinnfiguren* from Germany – is of leopard skins.

The experience of visiting a natural history museum or display consisted largely in meeting the dead and preserved bodies of exotic animals. We have seen how these animals made their way to the museums and it is now time to look at the industry of preservation and stuffing which enabled the animals to survive. Taxidermy was a massive industry in Victorian England. It is calculated that there are currently 1.2 million stuffed animals that were dead before 1901 in British museums. And these are the ones that have survived the culls of the 1960s and 1970s. In addition, there are many thousands, perhaps more than another million, of stuffed specimens in pubs, private houses, clubs and anywhere that there is a shelf to stand a case or a hook to hang a specimen. In Indian the firm of Van Ingen and Van Ingen was founded in Mysore in 1900 to service the world demand for Indian big game and also (and mainly) the demand of the local princes for trophies. It is estimated that they stuffed or preserved in some other way some 43,000 tigers and leopards. In their heyday they were turning out 400 tigers a year.

There was a major taxidermy display at the Great Exhibition where thirteen English and one German taxidermist had masterworks represented including a dodo reconstructed by Abraham Bartlett and a platypus stuffed by John Gould (whose work in taxidermy was not otherwise represented). But just a few miles away Gould had himself set up a display of stuffed hummingbirds in a purpose-built museum some sixty feet long and containing twenty-four cases each containing between five and fifteen birds displayed in naturalistic settings. Seventy-five thousand people came to see this show – which ran concurrently with the Great Exhibition – and paid sixpence (2.5p) each giving a gross return of £1,875 or roughly £115,000 in today's money. So you could visit the zoo and see both live and dead specimens on the same day and you paid separately for each experience. But while the experience of seeing the live animals was underpinned by the idea of seeing the wonders of the created natural world brought to the Imperial capital, the experience of seeing the stuffed specimens was more to do with wonderment at the capacity and skill of man as he exercised his mastery over both animals and Empire in the ultimate form of stealing not only the bodies of the subject creatures but also their lives.

Preserving animals was an essential skill for both the amateur and professional field naturalists as they had to get their specimens home in good shape. Birds were usually preserved as skins and capability in skin preparation was the foremost thing that John Gould looked for in his collectors. Indeed, the people who worked for Gould or Derby or Rothschild could not have stayed in business had they not been able to preserve in the field. Meek once sold Rothschild a single butterfly specimen for nearly £1,200. With that kind of money at stake no one would risk slapdash preservation. As we have seen, doing natural history in the field could be dangerous and it will come as no surprise to learn that field taxidermy also had its hazards. In 1898 the American taxidermist Carl Akerley was on an expedition in British Somaliland when he found himself fighting hand-to-hand with a furious leopard. He managed to strangle it and subsequently it no doubt joined the parade of stuffed animals exiting Akerley's workshop (he later became one of the first proponents of gorilla conservation and died of a fever while visiting a gorilla colony in the Congo). One notable amateur naturalist, taxidermist and the inventor of the nature reserve was the wildly eccentric Charles Waterton who had made his name in the late 1820s with some impressive accounts of his journeys to South America and in particular of the habits of sloths and vampire bats. In the course of his adventures he rode an alligator down a river bank somewhere in what is now Guyana. By the 1840s he was filling his house with stuffed specimens often of hybrid animals through which he created his own world of exotica including, for example, "the Nondescript" made from two red monkey skins deliberately stretched out of shape and various monsters such as a giant guinea pig with a human face and a tortoise shell. Waterton was important as his taxidermy technique was his own invention and the animals he preserved are actually hollow. But they have stood the test of time well and many can still be seen in Wakefield Museum.

The vast majority of stuffed specimens were, of course, of domestic animals and ranged from the mounted fox masks and the mighty glazed trout in the country houses to the individual specimens of squirrels in the vicar's study to the delicate arrangements of local birds under a glass dome in the middle-class parlour to the bizarre anthropomorphic displays produced at the very end of our period by the taxidermist Walter Potter (but also by others less well remembered). By 1900 there were eighteen major taxidermy companies operating in England, Scotland and Wales and a myriad of smaller ones. Most of the work involved working with local animals but just as the Victorian vet had, on occasion, to forget what he knew about cattle and work out what was wrong with the squire's elephant so the Victorian taxidermist had, on occasion, to work out what an animal he had never seen before might have looked liked. For example, Hutchings, which operated in Aberystwyth, worked mainly with local animals but they also stuffed at least one African Grey parrot and a case of hummingbirds. Sometimes they did a good job – for example the famous image of a kangaroo painted by Stubbs was done from an inflated skin – at other times the results were less happy such as the stuffed wombat in the Hancock Museum in Newcastle which is mounted in a rearing position unknown to wombat-kind. But the museums required specimens and, by 1901, the amalgamation of art and science represented by serious taxidermy had reached a point of perfection that enables us still today to see animals that last walked in the jungle or desert in the nineteenth century. The exotic was also to be found in palaeontology and the vogue for fossils and dinosaurs that swept Victorian England in the wake of Dean William Buckland's (Frank Buckland's father) work in particular led to many sites of reconstruction of these extinct exotic creatures most notably the magnificent life-size models made by Benjamin Waterhouse Hawkins.

However, this fashion, alongside the curious interest in sea serpents which became a minor craze in 1840s, is beyond the scope of this book. Living exotic animals are subject enough.

The dusty parade of stuffed animals completes this account of the ways in which people could encounter the exotic in Victorian England. Each site of encounter offered a different experience and each had its own fiscal and phenomenological economies. The theme of Empire links all the sites but so does the theme of loss and mourning. The thrills of the tearing of meat in Van Ambergh's cage or the thunder of bison hooves as Buffalo Bill's Wild West Show careered round the arena were only possible because of the capture and imprisonment of wild animals, some of which are now entirely lost to us and only preserved through nineteenth-century taxidermy. The liveliness of the menageries gives way to the orderliness of the zoological gardens which give way to the conspicuous consumption of the private collections which give way to the dismal relics of the natural history museums and the surrogate organs of taxidermy. In using the encounter with exotic animals to reconstruct a particular corner of Victorian culture and the tactility of Victorian experience we can go so far with human subjects but we can never go anywhere with the animals they gazed at. They are beyond our grasp entirely.

I have a clear memory of seeing Chi Chi the famous giant panda at London Zoo when I was a very small child. I remember the greyness of the day, the excitement of seeing the carts pulled by llamas and the camel rides – I must have been too small to go in them and certainly don't remember wanting to. I still had somewhere until quite recently some components of the model of the chimpanzees' tea party I was given, all still made of metal with, no doubt, fiendishly toxic lead-based paint (this may account for some of the *longeurs* of this book). I can remember Guy the gorilla and I can remember Chi Chi. All my childhood memories are a bit blurred as I was myopic and my coping strategies meant that no one – including me – realised until I was ten. But looking at the dates it seems to me that it is very unlikely that I saw Chi Chi. She arrived at the zoo in September 1958 and I am pretty sure I am talking about 1957. So I think the memory must be a synthesis of a later assumption that Chi Chi was part of that day at the zoo, of pictures of Chi Chi that were part of the fabric of England in the 1960s, and of a great desire to see a panda.

Chapter Seven

And that is the point. For most of my life my desire to have seen a panda has been so strong that I have lived very comfortably with a fabricated memory of having seen one. Somehow the incorporation of something as exotic as a panda into the memories that constitute my personality was important. I am completed by the memory in just the same way that the fabric of English society during the reign of Queen Victoria was somehow completed by the encounters which I have described in this book. I could, of course, now embark on a lengthy theoretical account based on the idea of the post-colonial, the other and the subaltern. But I won't because the facts of the matter (and the past is a collection of facts even if they are ungraspable) is actually very simple. The extension of the English mind onto the global stage of the Empire changed it just as it changed the things it encountered. The Empire was a dialogue and the dialogue constantly changed the terms of the languages in which it was conducted. To understand anything at all about the world it was necessary for my person from Grantham to meet a hippopotamus and that is why the Victorians, I suspect without knowing why, made sure that it was possible in so many different ways.

I doubt that exotic animals fabricate memories of seeing human beings.

Select Bibliography

This bibliography contains only the main secondary sources for this study. The numerous newspaper and magazines consulted are all cited in the main text. Similarly, I have not cited every one of the memoirs of animal collectors and naturalists which were also consulted: it is sufficient to say that almost everyone whose name appears in this book left at least one volume of memoirs and these can easily be sourced by the curious reader.

D. E. Allen, *The Victorian Fern Craze* (London, 1969)

J. Allen, *Samuel Johnson's Menagerie* (Norwich, 2002)

M. Allin, *Zarafa* (London, 1998)

R. D. Altick, *The Shows of London* (Cambridge MA, 1978)

S. Amato, "The White Elephant in London: an Episode of Trickery, Racism and Advertising", *Journal of Social History*, 43 (2009), pp. 31–66

I. Armstrong, *Victorian Glassworks* (Oxford, 2008)

S. Asma, *Stuffed Animals and Pickled Heads* (New York, 2003)

B. Assael, *The Circus and Victorian Society* (Virginia, 2005)

J. E. Auerbach, *The Great Exhibition of 1851* (New Haven, 1999)

R. Baird, *Goodwood: Art, Architecture, Sport and Family* (London, 2007)

E. Baratay & E. Hardouin-Fugier, *Zoo* (London, 2002)

L. Barber, *The Heyday of Natural History* (London, 1980)

J. Barrington-Johnson, *The Zoo* (London, 2005)

J. Bastin, *Natural History Drawings: The Complete William Farquhar Collection* (Singapore, 2010)

S. Basu, *Victoria and Abdul* (New Delhi, 2011)

M. Belozerskaya, *The Medici Giraffe* (New York, 2006)

P. Blanchard et al, *Human Zoos* (Liverpool, 2008)

W. Blunt, *The Ark in the Park* (London, 1976)

F. C. Bostock, *The Training of Wild Animals* (1911, repr. Amsterdam, 2003)

D. Bradbury, L. James and B. Sharratt (eds), *Performance and Politics in Popular Drama* (London, 1980)

Select Bibliography

W. Brasmer, "The Wild West and the Drama of Civilisation" in Mayer et al., op.cit, pp. 133–156

J. S. Bratton, "Theatre of War: the Crimea on the London Stage 1854–5" in D. Bradbury, L. James and B. Sharratt, op. cit., pp.119–138

T. Brown, et al., *An Illustrated History of Bristol Zoo Gardens* (Bristol, 2011)

R. K. Bruce, *Timothy the Tortoise* (London, 2004)

B. Brunner, *Bears* (New Haven, 2007)

D. Cadbury, *The Dinosaur Hunters* (London, 2000)

P. Chambers, *Jumbo* (London, 2007)

V. Chansigaud, *The History of Ornithology* (London, 2009)

D. Clifford, et al., *Positioning Victorian Science* (London, 2006)

D. Clode, *Continent of Curiosities* (Port Melbourne, 2006)

D. Collins, "The 'voice' of nature? Kookaburras, culture and Australian sound", *Journal of Australian Studies*, 35 (2011), pp.281–295

M. Conan, *Bourgeois and Aristocratic Cultural Encounters in Garden Art 1550–1850* (Dumbarton Oaks, 2002)

T. Cosslett, *Talking Animals in British Children's Fiction 1786–1914* (Aldershot, 2006)

C. de Courcy, *The Zoo Story* (Ringwood VIC, 1995)

C. de Courcy, *Evolution of a Zoo* (Melbourne, 2003)

C. de Courcy, *Dublin Zoo: An Illustrated History* (Wilton, 2009)

H. Cowie, "Elephants, Education and Entertainment", *Journal of the History of Collections*, 23 (2012), pp. 1–13

P. Cribb and M. Tibbs, *A Very Victorian Passion* (London, 2004)

A. Crosby, *Ecological Imperialism* (Cambridge, 1986)

S. P. Dance, *A History of Shell Collecting* (Leiden, 1986)

S. P. Dance, "Hugh Cuming (1791–1865) Prince of Collectors", *Journal of the Society Biblphy Natural History*, 9 (1980), pp. 477–501

M. Diamond, *Victorian Sensation* (London, 2004)

D. Donald, *Picturing Animals in Britain 1750–1850* (New Haven, 2007)

T. R. Dunlap, "Remaking the land: The Acclimatization Movement and Anglo Ideas of Nature", *Journal of World History*, 8 (1997), pp. 303–319

N. Durbach, "London, Capital of Exotic Exhibitions from 1830–1860" in Blanchard (2208), pp. 81-88

E. Ellis, *Rare and Curious* (Carlton, 2010)

F. Fan, *British Naturalists in Qing China* (Cambridge, MA, 2004)

M. Ferguson, *Animal Advocacy and Englishwomen 1780–1900* (Ann Arbor, 1998)

S. Festing, "Menageries and the Landscape Garden", *Journal of Garden History*, 8 (1988), pp. 104–117

Select Bibliography

C. Finney, *Paradise Revealed* (Melbourne, 1993)

C. Fisher (ed.), *A Passion for Natural History* (Liverpool, 2002)

J. Flanders, *The Victorian House* (London, 2003)

J. Flanders, *Consuming Passions* (London, 2006)

E. Fuller, *The Dodo* (Boston, 2003)

B. T. Gates, *Kindred Nature* (Chicago, 1998)

G. H. Gerzina, *Black Victorians, Black Victoriana* (New York, 2003)

T. Gott, "An Iron Maiden for Melbourne", *The La Trobe Journal*, 81 (2008), pp. 53–69

L. Granfield, *The Circus 1870–1950* (London, 2009)

J. Gregory, *Of Victorians and Vegetarians* (London, 2007)

T. Griffiths, *Hunters and Collectors* (Cambridge, 1997)

A. Grihault, *The Dodo* (Mauritius, 2005)

J. Ham and M. Senior (eds), *Animal Acts* (London, 1997)

D. Hancocks, *A Different Nature* (Berkeley, 2001)

L. Harding, *Elephant Story* (Jefferson, N. C., 2000)

D. Hart-Davis, *Audubon's Elephant* (London, 2003)

M. Henniger-Voss, *Animals in Human History* (Rochester NY, 2002)

A. D. Hippisley Coxe, "Equestrian Drama and the Circus" in D. Bradbury, L. James and B. Sharratt, op.cit., pp. 109–118

P. Hoare, *Leviathan* (London, 2008)

J. Hoorn, *Reframing Darwin* (Melbourne, 2009)

S. Jackson, *Koala* (Crow's Nest, 2007)

S. Jackson and K. Vernes, *Kangaroo* (Crow's Nest, 2010)

R. Jones, "The Sight of Creatures Strange to our Clime: London Zoo and the Consumption of the Exotic", *Journal of Victorian Culture*, 2 (1997), pp. 1–26

L. Kalof, *Looking at Animals in Human History* (London, 2007)

V. N. Kisling (ed.), *Zoo and Aquarium History* (Boca Raton, 2001)

D. Kumar, "The Evolution of Colonial Science in India: Natural History and the East India Company" in Mackenzie (1990) op. cit., pp. 51–66

L. Lambton, *Beastly Buildings* (London, 1985)

L. Lambton, *Palaces for Pigs* (London, 2011)

M. J. Largen, "Taxonomically and Historically Significant Specimens of Mammals in the Merseyside County Museums, Liverpool", *Journal of Mammology*, 66 (1985), pp. 412–418

B. Larson, *Art of Evolution* (Oxford, 2009)

C. Lever, *They Dined on Eland* (London, 1992)

L. Lippincott & A. Blühm, *Fierce Friends* (London, 2005)

Select Bibliography

G. Loisel, *Histoire des Ménageries de l'Antiquité à Nos Jours*, 3 volumes (Paris, 1912)

C. F. Loughney, "Collecting the Colonies: Victorian Museums and the Creation of Other Landscapes", Paper Presented at the Forum UNESCO University and Heritage 10th International Seminar "Cultural Landscapes in the 21st Century" Newcastle upon Tyne, 11–16 April 2005 Revised: July 2006

S. Lyons, "Swimming at the Edge of Scientific Respectability: Sea Serpents in the Victorian Era", in D. Clifford, et al., op. cit., pp. 31–44

D. Mayer and K. Richards (eds), *Western Popular Theatre* (London, 1977)

R. McDowall, *Gamekeepers for the Nation* (Christchurch, 1994)

J. Mackenzie, *Imperialism and Popular Culture* (Manchester, 1986)

J. Mackenzie, *The Empire of Nature* (Manchester, 1988)

J. Mackenzie (ed.), *Imperialism and the Natural World* (Manchester, 1990)

J. Mackenzie (ed.), *The Victorian Vision* (London, 2001)

J. L. Middlemiss, *A Zoo on Wheels* (Winshill, 1987)

W. Moore, *The Knife Man* (London, 2005)

G. Morey, *The Lincoln Kangaroos* (London, 1962)

P. A. Morris, *Rowland Ward, Taxidermist to the World* (Ascot, 2003)

P. A. Morris, *Edward Gerrard and Sons, A Taxidermy Memoir* (Ascot, 2004)

P. A. Morris, *Van Ingen and Van Ingen, Artists in Taxidermy* (Ascot, 2006)

P. A. Morris, *Hutchings: The Aberystwyth Taxidermists 1860–1942* (Ascot, 2007)

P. A. Morris, *Walter Potter and his Museum of Curious Taxidermy* (Ascot, 2008)

D. D. Morse & M. A. Danahay (eds), *Victorian Animal Dreams* (Aldershot, 2007)

A. Moyal, *Platypus* (Crow's Nest, 2001)

A. Moyal, *Koala* (Collingwood, 2008)

B. Mullan & G. Marvin, *Zoo Culture* (Urbana, 1999)

N. Murray, *Lives of the Zoo: Charismatic Animals in the Social Worlds of the Zoological Gardens of London*, unpublished Ph.D thesis, Indiana University, 2004

H. Nicholls, *The Way of the Panda* (London, 2010)

H. J. Noltie, *Raffles' Ark Redrawn* (London, 2009)

P. Olsen, *Upside Down World* (Canberra, 2010)

D. Opitz, "This House is a Temple of Research: Country House Centres for Late Victorian Science", in Clifford, op. cit., pp. 143–156

D. Owen, *Thylacine* (Crow's Nest, 2003)

D. Owen and D. Pemberton, *Tasmanian Devil* (Crow's Nest, 2005)

J. M. Packard, *Farewell in Splendour* (London, 1995)

R. Paddle, *The Last Tasmanian Tiger* (Cambridge, 2000)

I. Parsonsons, *The Australian Ark* (Collingwood, 1998)

Select Bibliography

G. M. Pflugfelder & B. L. Walker, *JAPAnimals* (Ann Arbor, 2005)

J. M. Picker, *Victorian Soundscapes* (Oxford, 2003)

C. Plumb, *Exotic Animals in Eighteenth-Century Britain*, unpublished Ph.D thesis (University of Manchester, 2010)

R. Poignant, *Professional Savages* (Sydney, 2004)

P. Raby, *Bright Paradise* (London, 1996)

T. Richards, *The Commodity Culture of Victorian England* (London, 1990)

G. Ridley, *Clara's Grand Tour* (London, 2004)

H. Ritvo, *The Animal Estate* (London, 1987)

H. Ritvo, *The Mermaid and the Platypus* (Cambridge MA, 1997)

C. E. Rix, *Royal Zoological Society of South Australia* ((Netley, SA, 1978)

L. E. Robbins, *Elephant Slaves and Pampered Pets* (Baltimore, 2002)

M. Rosenthal, C. Tauber & E. Uhlir, *The Ark in the Park* (Urbana, 2003)

N. Rothfels, *Savages and Beasts* (Baltimore, 2002)

N. Rothfels, "Catching Animals" in M. Henniger-Voss, *op. cit.*, 182–228

M. Rothschild, *Walter Rothschild* (London, 2008)

R. Russell, *The Business of Nature* (Canberra, 2011)

M. A. Salmon, *The Aurelian Legacy: British Butterflies and their Collectors* (Berkeley, 2000)

M. StLeon, *Circus: the Australian Story* (Melbourne 2011)

L. Sanders, *Old Kew, Chiswick and Kensington* (London, 1910)

G. Sanger, *Seventy Years a Showman* (New York, 1910)

D. Scarisbrick, *Scottish Jewellery: A Victorian Passion* (London, 2009)

E. Scigliano, *Love, War and Circuses* (London, 2004)

J. Simons, *Rossetti's Wombat* (London, 2008)

L. Schiebinger, *Plants and Empire* (Cambridge, MA, 2004)

K. Scrivens & S. Smith, *Manders Shows and Menageries* (Newcastle under Lyme, no date, 2008?)

L. Slade, et al., *Curious Colony* (Newcastle, 2010)

J. Smith, *Charles Darwin and Victorian Visual Culture* (Cambridge, 2006)

M. Steele & M. Benbough-Jackson, "Liverpool 1886: Selling the City of Ships", CHARM Proceedings 2011, pp. 182–193

R. Stott, *Theatres of Glass* (London, 2003)

R. Strahan, *Beauty and the Beast* (Chipping Norton, NSW, 1991)

M. Sweet, *Inventing the Victorians* (London, 2002)

J. E. Taylor, *The Aquarium* (Edinburgh, 1910)

I. Tree, *The Bird Man* (London, 1991)

E. S. Turner, *All Heaven in a Rage* (London, 1964, new ed., Fontwell, 1992)

J. Uglow, *Nature's Engraver* (London, 2006)

Select Bibliography

R. Verdi, *The Parrot in Art* (London, 2007)

G. Vevers, *London's Zoo* (London, 1976)

F. Watson, *The Year of the Wombat* (London, 1974)

S. Whittingham, *Fern Fever* (London, 2012)

M. H. Winter, "Popular Theatre and Popular Art", in Mayer et al., op.cit, pp. 229–238

P. Womack, *Improvement and Romance* (London, 1989)

S. J. Woolfall, "The History of the 13th Earl of Derby's Menagerie and Aviary at Knowsley Hall", *Archives of Natural History*, 19 (1990), pp. 1–47

J. Yallop, *Magpies, Squirrels and Thieves* (London, 2011)

M. Zgórniak, "Fremiet's Gorillas: Why Do They Carry Off Women?" *Artibus et Historiae*, 27 (2006), pp. 219–237

Website

http://www.nfa.dept.shef.ac.uk/jungle/index.html

This is the website of Sheffield University's "Sheffield Jungle" project. Here Dr Ian Trowell and his team have reconstructed in painstaking detail Bostock's "Jungle" in its various manifestations in Sheffield between 1910 and 1913.

Index

Index

Index

Index

Index

Index

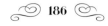

Index

Index

Index

Index

Index

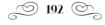

Index

Index